The
Heart and Soul
of Imitating
Christ

The Heart and Soul of Imitating Christ

A Fresh Look at the Thomas à Kempis Classic

MITCH FINLEY

Liguori
LIGUORI, MISSOURI

Imprimi Potest:
Thomas D. Picton, C.Ss.R.
Provincial, Denver Province
The Redemptorists

Published by Liguori Publications
Liguori, Missouri
www.liguori.org

Library of Congress Cataloging-in-Publication Data

Finley, Mitch.
    The heart and soul of imitating Christ : a fresh look at the Thomas à Kempis classic / Mitch Finley.—1st ed.
        p.   cm.
    ISBN 0-7648-1342-0
    1. Meditations. I. Imitatio Christi. II. Title.
BV4832.3.F56   2006
242—dc22   2005028324

Liguori Publications, a nonprofit corporation, is an apostolate of the Redemptorists. To learn more about the Redemptorists, visit *Redemptorists.com.*

Printed in the United States of America
10 09 08 07 06   5 4 3 2 1
First edition

Contents

Introduction

In 1966, I was a twenty-year-old United States Navy petty officer third class stationed at the Marine Corps Air Station at Kaneohe Bay, Hawaii. When the sun set on clear, cloudless evenings the view of the Pali—the mountain range that divides the island of Oahu into its windward and leeward sides—from our barracks was spectacular. On many occasions I watched the sun reflected on the mountains and my heart delivered itself of a wordless prayer of praise and thanksgiving.

I sometimes think that my Catholic faith began to grow into young adulthood during such moments. It was then that I learned, in ways impossible to put into words, that God's love was more than a theory, far more than words. I began to learn that God's love truly is the unconditional, always-reliable, constantly trustworthy love of the father of Jesus and our father, too. It was then that I began to learn that words such as these are but a feeble attempt to express the wordless knowledge that filled my heart as I watched the wonderful sunsets that the windward side of Oahu offers.

Because of such experiences, I began to read in order to better understand what I experienced, and one of the first books that, by some mysterious grace, fell into my hands was the famous autobiography of Thomas Merton, *The Seven Storey Mountain*.

Not long after his conversion to Catholicism in 1938, Merton happened to meet a traveling Hindu monk named Bramachari. I was astonished when I read that Bramachari did not urge Merton to read the various classics of the eastern religions—although he would do so, in depth, over the years. Instead, he advised Merton to read the spiritual classics of his own western Christian heritage, including Saint Augustine's *Confessions* and Thomas à Kempis' *The Imitation of Christ*.

The first opportunity I had to search out a copy of *The Imitation*

I did so. As it happened, I found an inexpensive paperback copy in a bookstore on a side street in Waikiki. I still have that book some forty years later, its cheap pages yellow and musty with the passing years. I have other translations, too, but that old pocket-sized paperback never fails to evoke a special warmth for me because of the countless times I have turned and read its pages. Years later, having earned undergraduate and graduate degrees in theology, I would hold *The Imitation* at arm's length using the tools of a historical-critical approach to read the words of Thomas à Kempis with something of a student's objectivity. My first few readings of *The Imitation*, however, would never leave me and would condition all subsequent readings and all my later studying of its wisdom.

Something told me, from the first time I read its opening paragraphs, that here was a wisdom that transcends time and places. Granted, it was a good thing that I later made the effort to read the sentences of *The Imitation* with some critical distance, for it is clearly possible to gather mistaken notions from it after all these centuries. As it turned out, however, a bit of academic objectivity only increased my admiration for the salubrious wisdom to be found in *The Imitation*.

The Imitation of Christ, written in the early fifteenth century, is with no exaggeration often called the most widely read devotional book ever and the most widely read book of any kind, second only to the Bible. Saint Thomas More (1478–1535), Lord Chancellor of England under King Henry VIII who died at Henry's command rather than deny his Catholic faith, said that it was one of the three books that everyone should read. Saint Ignatius Loyola (1491–1556), founder of the Jesuits, read a chapter of *The Imitation* each day. As a seminarian, Angelo Roncalli—the future Pope John XXIII—copied excerpts from it in his private journal. Dorothy Day, co-founder of the Catholic Worker movement, wrote that "it followed me through my days. Again and again I came across copies of it and the reading of it brought me comfort." Echoing the words of Saint Paul, *The Imitation of Christ* encourages the reader to put on Christ and pursue a life of authentic faith in order to find peace and fulfillment.

The Imitation's exact date of publication is impossible to determine, but scholars agree that it was in circulation by the year 1427 and popular throughout Western Europe. Originally written in Latin, it was soon translated into Dutch, German, French, English, and Italian. Printed editions appeared toward the end of the 1400s, and some two thousand editions and translations have appeared since it was first set in then-newly-invented movable type. Today, more than twenty editions are available in English. In addition, large print, Braille, and audio editions are readily obtainable.

Since its appearance over five hundred years ago, some thirty-five different people have been suggested as author of *The Imitation*. Scholarly consensus, however, continues to support the traditional author, Thomas à Kempis. Thomas Haemerken, born in Kempen, the Rhineland, in 1370, was the second son of John and Gertrude Haemerken. Though peasants, the Haemerkens managed to send Thomas to schools in Deventer, which were operated by the Brothers of the Common Life, a Christian community for laymen and some clergy. Thomas thought he would join the Brothers of the Common life, but in 1399 he chose instead Mount Saint Agnes, a newly founded monastery of the Canons Regular of Saint Augustine, in Zwolle, the Netherlands. His older brother, John, was prior there.

Little is known of Thomas's activities in the monastery at Mount Saint Agnes, except that he copied manuscripts and composed numerous works, including some lives of the saints. Twice he served as subprior, and for a time he was master of novices. Thomas died on August 8, 1471, in the monastery where he had spent virtually his entire adult life.

Thomas à Kempis evidently relied on many sources in writing *The Imitation of Christ*. About one thousand direct and indirect quotations from the Bible have been identified, as well as numerous unacknowledged "borrowings" from masters of the spiritual life, including Saint Bernard of Clairvaux, William of Saint Thierry, and the anonymously authored *Cloud of Unknowing*. Most directly, however, *The Imitation* is rooted in a spiritual renewal movement, the *Devotio Moderna*, which appeared in Western Europe in the last decades of the fifteenth century, a time when much corruption had found its way into the Church. Thomas "called all to serious pursuit of the path Christ had walked," wrote Lutheran historian of Christianity Martin Marty, "in marked contradiction of their times."

The idea of "imitating" Christ is a theme central to the Christian life. This idea simply means that all Christians are called to conform their lives to that of Christ. "Imitation" is not the same as "discipleship," which refers to following Christ. Rather, the "imitation" of Christ refers to conformity to the person and example of Jesus so as to manifest in one's own person the presence of the risen Christ in the world. In other words, *The Imitation* is about transformation in Christ. This idea originated with Saint Paul who speaks often, in his New Testament letters, of life in Christ. For Paul, baptism is the initiation of the believer into the dying and rising of Jesus. As Paul wrote in his Letter to the Galatians, "I have been crucified with Christ; and it is no longer I who live, but it is Christ who lives in me" (2:19b). Thus, martyrs in the early Church, those who died for their faith, were honored as imitators of Christ.

"Imitation of Christ" does not mean an attempt to reproduce literally the actions or lifestyle of Jesus as presented in the gospels. Rather, "imitation" refers to life in this world as graced and guided by the Holy Spirit. All forms of the Christian life—married, single, ordained priesthood, and vowed religious life—embody a call to imitate Christ, to be conformed to Jesus who is the way, the truth and the life (see John 14:6).

The Imitation consists of four separate books, only the first of which was originally titled *De Imitatione Christi*. In Book I, Thomas reflects on the problems and temptations to be expected in the early stages of the life of Christian faith. The theme of separation from secular society—appropriate to a monastic vocation but not without meaningful implications for any Christian life—dominates, and Thomas emphasizes the need to contemplate the example of Christ.

Book II is quieter in tone, with more emphasis on the peace to be gained from a spiritual detachment from the activities and enthusiasms of "the world"—what we today might call "the dominant popular culture" or, in some cases, "secular society." Thomas turns over and over to the inner joy to be found through authentic faith. But this inner peace cannot be obtained without embracing self-sacrifice for the sake of God and neighbor, Thomas writes, and so Christians must expect the discomfort of self-denial and the inconvenience of self-discipline, all for a deeper freedom and a deeper joy than any "the world" can offer.

In Book III, the author's style shifts to one of dialogue between the follower of Christ and the risen Lord. Spiritual comfort is the main theme. The spirit of humility and self-effacement is uppermost. Conscious of his own unimportance, the disciple is even more aware of the love of the Lord who cares for him in spite of his unworthiness.

The final book of *The Imitation* has the greatest internal unity due to its single theme: the Eucharist. For Thomas à Kempis, the consecrated bread of the Eucharist is a sacramental medicine, "the health of soul and body, the remedy for every sickness of the spirit," as well as a focus of attentive devotion.

Betty I. Knott, in the introduction to her English translation published in 1963 (the edition I bought in that little Waikiki book shop in 1966), wrote that *The Imitation* "is a distillation of the atmosphere, beliefs, and ideals of a whole religious movement—the mysticism and piety of the Netherlands and the Rhineland in the fourteenth and fifteenth centuries...." Because *The Imitation* is a product of a culture and an age long past, it makes special demands on the modern reader who needs to remember the historical, cultural, and religious contexts from which it emerged. It is also prudent to be on the lookout for manifestations of simple human shortsightedness. The fifteenth century, no less than the twenty-first, had its weaknesses as well as its virtues.

In his 1950 classic, *Enthusiasm*, Monsignor Ronald Knox remarked on "the semi-Jansenist atmosphere" of *The Imitation*, "which escapes so many readers." For Thomas à Kempis, "the world" and "the things of the world" are first of all a danger to the spiritual life. He seems to undervalue the impact of the Incarnation and Redemption on the created order and human societies and cultures. Such an approach is to be expected given the theological perspectives and piety of his time. Still, the modern reader does well to respect the perennial truth of Thomas's perspective, for the notion that the Christian is called to live "in but not of the world" is basic to Christian faith with roots that go back at least as far as the Letters of Saint Paul and the Gospel of John.

Thomas à Kempis is sometimes mistakenly quoted to support religious anti-intellectualism. One of the most famous passages from *The Imitation* used to support religious anti-intellectualism reads, "I would rather be able to feel compunction in my heart than be able to define it." Remember, however, that Thomas was trained in the *Devotio Moderna*, a tradition that placed great value on the intellect and academic pursuits. Famous lines from *The Imitation*, such as "Learned arguments do not make a man holy...," take for granted the value and goodness of the intellectual component of faith but caution the reader to guard against academic pursuits divorced from the love of God and neighbor. The last thing Thomas à Kempis would have wanted was to denigrate the intellectual life. This book makes this perspective explicit.

It is the purpose of this book to present the wisdom of *The Imitation of Christ* in terms more relevant to life in the twenty-first century. This book is not another translation of *The Imitation of Christ*. Neither is it a paraphrase. Rather, while retaining Thomas's original outline and purpose, this book is an attempt to write *The Imitation of Christ* as if it were being written today. It uses contemporary theological perspectives in an attempt to convey the wisdom of *The Imitation* in ways that will make the most sense for everyday Christians who live in the twenty-first century rather than the fifteenth. Because, as we acknowledged above, Thomas à Kempis wrote from the cultural and theological perspectives of his time, it remains to his credit that his book continues to touch the hearts and lives of countless readers. All the same, it is easy to misinterpret what Thomas's words mean in today's world. Therefore, a book such as this one may be of value for readers who find themselves perplexed by even the most contemporary translations of *The Imitation*. At the same time, Thomas sometimes tends to go on at unnecessary length. I have tried to say what needs to be said without belaboring the point.

This book follows the structure and content of *The Imitation of Christ*—except for a few omitted chapters—saying what Thomas à Kempis said in words and ways that readers in the twenty-first century will find more easily understandable and more meaningful. The ultimate intention of this book remains, however, the same as that of the original, namely, to help the reader better understand that love alone, the kind of love that is rock-solid and reliable regardless of circumstances, gives life meaning and purpose, and this love alone makes it possible to find both God, one's deepest self, and the meaning of life.

BOOK I

Some Good Advice on the Life of Christian Faith

Following Christ in a Sometimes Phony World

"I am the light of the world. Whoever follows me will never walk in darkness but will have the light of life."
JOHN 8:12

These words of Jesus in the Gospel of John form the heart, soul, and foundation of any Christian life. If we seek enlightenment, true spiritual freedom, and liberation from hardness of heart, let us ponder these words and reflect upon the mind of Jesus Christ as presented to us in Scripture and the Tradition of the Church. Let us meditate upon the four gospels, seek inspiration from the lives of the saints, and attend to the words of thoughtful believers in our own time and to the teachings of the shepherds of the Church.

Sometimes people think that if they have a clever mind, or academic degrees, or if they are "popular," that makes them better than others. Such people forget that they are what they are, no more and no less. People who boast and brag are a pain to be around. Even people who keep their feelings of superiority hidden most of the time are likely to show their true colors in moments of stress or conflict with others. The truth is that the only fulfilling life is a life based on self-forgetfulness and empathy toward others; indeed, this is the only life that is compatible with Christian faith.

It is futile to allow your main concern to be to gain as much material comfort and financial security as possible. It is futile, too, to think of yourself as better than others. It is foolish to do everything you can to live a *long* life—good nutrition, regular exercise, and so forth—while at the same time giving little attention to living a *good* life. A good life comes from making choices that help you to love God and neighbor in practical, everyday ways, which is far more important than trying to satisfy a craving for an affluent lifestyle and financial forms of security, a craving that can never be satisfied.

Remember that whenever we long for anything, really, our ultimate longing is for a loving union with God, with family and friends, and with those who are less fortunate than ourselves. It's a big mistake to think that more possessions and a bigger annual income will free us from our deepest craving—which God alone can satisfy.

Remember the old saying from the Book of Ecclesiastes, in the Hebrew Scriptures, which declares that "the eye is not satisfied with seeing, / or the ear filled with hearing" (1:8). These words mean that if we want the joy and peace that are lasting, we need to cultivate emotional distance from the things the popular culture offers that give a false joy and a peace that never lasts. At the same time, we need to remember that the world is a sacrament of God. Much that we find in the popular culture is good. The skill we need to cultivate is the ability to discern the difference between what in the popular culture is good and what is not.

CHAPTER 2

The Proper Uses of Knowledge and Education

Everyone has an in-born desire for knowledge and understanding. This is only natural. But an obscure person who is truly devoted to the love of God and neighbor, even if most people think of this person as unimportant, is more valuable in the eyes of God than a genius who never gives a thought to the love of God and never asks the ultimate questions: Where did I come from? What is my purpose here? What is my ultimate destiny? Even if I am the greatest thinker of my generation, what good does it do me in the presence of God, who cares only for how well I have tried to love him and how well I have tried to be of caring service to the people around me?

The more knowledge and skills you gain, the more God expects of you when it comes to living a good life. A highly educated or highly trained person needs to remember the importance of balancing his or her life with regular prayer and unselfish service to others that brings no financial reward. For most people marriage and family life bring more than enough opportunities to do this, especially during the child-rearing years. But we must look for ways to integrate prayer and service into whatever life we find ourselves living. Only a prayerful life of service can be a truly Christian life. Yet remember that you do not live in a monastery, so your practice of prayer must fit the life you live in the real, knockabout world.

CHAPTER 3

How to Integrate Faith With What You Learned in School

How happy is the person who learns from truth itself, knowing that Christ himself is truth. When it comes to using the brain God gave us, our natural inclinations often get us into trouble. What good does it do to get into useless arguments with other people when there is no possibility of us proving them wrong or of them proving us wrong? Also, it makes no sense at all to neglect prayer and the love of God and neighbor in order to occupy ourselves with mere escapist forms of entertainment or diversionary activities. God expects us to use the gifts and talents he has given us and not let them go to waste.

The greater our awareness becomes of how close God is to us, and the more single-minded we become about our faith, the better our hearts will comprehend the overwhelming mystery of God's love. For the deeper our consciousness of how close God is to us and how passionately God loves us, the better will we grasp the meaning of faith.

Those whose faith permeates their whole life, whose awareness of God's constant loving presence is itself constant, these people will have no trouble keeping their priorities straight. They will not be distracted by worries and anxieties, nor will they allow their hearts to be fearful for long. For authentic faith helps you to turn away from being self-centered. What greater hindrance to freedom and peace can there be than to be centered on self?

At the same time, always remember that there needs to be regular times when you leave aside your daily activities and concerns in order to have time for prayer, to reinvigorate yourself spiritually. You can't share a new idea unless you take the time to read a book. You can't share your faith unless you make time to focus on your intimacy with the risen Lord.

The person of true Christian faith makes plans and does not allow worries, fears, or a desire for wealth to control his or her heart. Rather, the person of faith does what must be done, and what should be done, and leaves the results to God. For the person of faith, it is enough to know that he or she did the best that could be done.

The most difficult thing in life is to live a balanced, integrated life. Too many people allow themselves to be controlled by fears and anxieties about the future. Our main project in life should be to do our best and trust completely in God, never giving in to fear, anxiety, worry, and the illusion that all the answers in life are to be found in financial forms of security or in the approval of others.

Both formal education and "the school of hard knocks" have their value, to be sure. Both kinds of learning are good and come from God. However, learning in itself is useless apart from a lively Christian faith and a dedication to living a good life each and every day. Without this dedication your life will be empty, and you will be frustrated and unhappy.

If only we could be as ready to live every moment as people of faith as we are to give in to worry and fear. If only we were as ready to trust in God's love as we are to argue about our theological or political opinions. There is no question that our Father in heaven cares not a bit about our opinions, only about what we have done and are doing to act on our love for God and neighbor.

I'd like to know where are all the worries and fears that occupied you and caused you anguish in former times? Other anxieties have taken their place. What about the teachers and authors of popular books who were so influential a few years ago? Today other teachers and authors have taken their place. Only the love of God and his grace remain constant, so why not focus more on faith and trust than on fear and worry?

Is it not astonishing how quickly fashions fade? Is it not astonishing how what's "in" is different now than it was a few years ago? Is it not amusing how quickly celebrities come and go? Yet the dominant popular culture fawns upon the latest trends and the latest celebrities as if they will last forever. Could fashions, trends, and celebrities stand for truth and goodness instead of standing for false values and empty ideas.

So many end up with sad, meaningless lives because they make choices—often early in life—that Scripture and sacred Tradition reveal to be self-destructive. So many choose to ignore traditional moral and ethical standards in favor of what "everyone" is doing. Then they find their lives on a downward spiral from which it is difficult to escape. Does it not make sense to pay attention to the moral values that emerged from many generations of human experience? Does it not make sense to do this rather than to arrogantly assume that the present generation has discovered that Scripture and sacred Tradition are full of error and darkness? But no, so many do just this to their eventual regret and great unhappiness. They care little for the wisdom of Scripture and sacred Tradition and even less for a life dedicated to the love of God and neighbor, choosing instead a life centered on self and on immediate gratification.

God, our loving father, you who are truth itself, draw me to yourself in unconditional love. Often I grow tired of the frantic activity in my life. Too often I seek rest and relief in things and activities that are empty. You alone can fill the great emptiness in my deepest center. Help me to turn away more often from the distractions I turn to for relief, and help me turn to you instead. Fill my heart with your love alone.

Be Charitable in Both Word and Action

Be cautious about believing everything you hear. Whenever someone says something negative about another person, consider his or her words carefully while you are prayerfully present to God. For some reason, we're often more ready to believe and speak trash about someone than to believe or speak good of him or her. The ideal to aim for is to reject all negative talk about others until it becomes more than mere gossip. Remember human weakness when it comes to savoring tasty morsels of gossip, whether they are true or not.

It's a sign of a mature heart to think before acting. Likewise, the spiritually mature person is ready to abandon any opinion when it proves to be wrong. Don't believe everything bad you hear about others, and at all costs avoid repeating what you heard. Diarrhea of the mouth usually indicates constipation of the brain.

Consider yourself fortunate if you can find someone with much wisdom and common sense. This is the person from whom you should seek guidance and advice. In many instances, it's better to follow such a person's suggestions than to ignore what he or she says. Sometimes the worst step you can take is to follow your own inclinations without getting input from someone older and more experienced than you are. Cultivate humility, which is not the same thing as groveling. Rather, true humility means acting on the truth about yourself. If you are gifted in some way, don't pretend that you're not. If you have weaknesses, don't act as if don't. Simply be who you are without bragging and without becoming anyone else's doormat. The more genuinely humble you are, and the more you pray for God's guidance, the more practical, everyday wisdom you will have, and the deeper your peace will become.

CHAPTER 5

Learn to Read the Scriptures
With Mind and Heart

In the holy Scriptures we seek the truth about our relationships with God, other people, and the whole of creation. But remember that you can't merely pick up a Bible and start reading as if it was all written last week. Especially when you first begin to read the Bible, it's just as important to read about the Bible as it is to read the Bible itself. It's important to understand the many implications of the fact that the scriptural documents were written in many times and many places, in cultures very different from our own. In order to understand what a particular Bible passage means today, you must first have some idea of what it meant to those who first read it many centuries ago. It's important to find out as much as you can about what the inspired human author of a given biblical document intended to say in the first place. Then you can begin to understand what the Scriptures say to us today.

Read good books on spirituality and contemporary religious issues, but be careful because, for example, there are more than a few crackpot authors ready to sell you religious nonsense based on ignorant assumptions about the Scriptures. In particular, the New Testament's Book of Revelation lends itself easily to irresponsible interpretations.

If you wish to benefit the most from reading and praying with the Scriptures, realize that what matters is that you remain open to the living Word of God, which is far deeper than and transcends the human words of Scripture. The Bible isn't an end in itself, it's a kind of "sacrament" of God's presence among us. We don't worship the Bible, we worship the God who inspired the Bible. Read with an informed mind and in the context of God's unconditional love for you and for all. Don't try to impress others with your knowledge of the Scriptures. Ask your questions, and then be open to God's Word, which is both in and far deeper than the Bible. Don't get sidetracked by debatable questions. Listen, also, to the wisdom to be found in sacred Tradition—which includes the Eucharist and the other sacraments and rituals of the Church; the lives and words of the saints, both ancient and modern; and the thoughts of contemporary thinkers. Ponder, too, the teachings of the Church's legitimate teaching authorities without, however, attributing infallibility to every word on issues from official Church sources.

CHAPTER 6

Learn to Recognize
What *Really* Brings Peace

Whenever you find yourself saying, "I *must* have that," learn to recognize that whenever you want something with a powerful craving, you immediately become unhappy. Don't let your happiness and sense of contentment depend upon anything outside of yourself, and certainly not upon whether or not you have this or that possession. Only those who put love of God and neighbor first have real peace of mind and heart.

Anyone who must have the latest convenience items, the latest "toys," in order to be happy, will never be happy. Anyone who is weak in spirit and must have all kinds of comforts and conveniences, soon finds that true peace and happiness seem farther and farther away. Such people are often depressed and unpleasant to be around, so they find that they have no friends. They find that they grow irritable and even angry when someone suggests that they may not need the things they say they "must" have in order to be happy.

The more we give in to mass media advertising, which constantly tells us that we need things that no one really needs, the unhappier we become. And giving in to cultural pressures to accumulate more and more comforts, conveniences, and possessions makes us more unhappy, not happier. Only by resisting such pressures can true peace of mind and heart be found. Peace is found only in one who truly prefers the love of God and neighbor to all else.

CHAPTER 7

Trust in God and
Avoid Unhealthy Pride

It's foolish to put your ultimate trust in anything but the love of God, for everything else will disappoint you sooner or later. For example, if you are married your spouse will never become a perfect person who never irritates or disappoints you. Only if you are deeply rooted in God's love will you be able to tolerate your husband's or wife's limitations and failures for fifty or sixty years. If God's love is your ultimate source of peace, you will have the patience and forgiveness you need for a happy marriage. Then you will have the resources you need to serve one another for the love of Jesus Christ.

In the long and the short run, do the best you can and then put all your trust in God. Do what you really can do, and God will take over from there. On this advice you can rely completely.

If you are wealthy, don't flaunt or brag about it. If you have friends who are rich and powerful, never mention it unless you can't avoid doing so. But give thanks daily for your faith and for God's unconditional love. Be ready to share your faith with others, primarily by serving and caring for them, but with your words, too, if it becomes necessary and helpful to do so. Words are not as important as actions.

If you're handsome or beautiful, strong and healthy, don't give it a second thought. It takes very little time, or a simple accident, for physical attractiveness to become disfigured. Middle age and old age come to us all, and your body is temporary. Also, don't brag about any talents or skills you may have, but in your private prayers give thanks to God and ask him to help you use the talents and skills he gave you to properly to serve and care for others in appropriate ways.

Don't think of yourself as better than anyone else, but also don't think of yourself as inferior to anyone else. You are who you are, no more and no less. Don't brag about your accomplishments, for God's standards are sometimes different from human standards. More often than you might think, what impresses other people God has no interest in at all. And what matters to God is often dismissed as unimportant by people.

Choose Your Companions Carefully

Know with whom you're talking before you open your heart to someone. Better to talk about your personal concerns with someone who is older, more experienced, and filled with love for God. Don't be too quick to hang around with people you don't know well yet or who seem foolish or too ready to engage in timewasting activities. Avoid those who abuse drugs or alcohol. Avoid people who show little or no respect for God, other people, or the natural world. No good can come from hanging around with such people. Also, don't flatter those who have more money or a more affluent lifestyle than you have, and don't fall all over yourself to be in the presence of people who are celebrities or otherwise important and influential in the eyes of the world at large. They are just people.

Go out of your way to spend time with people who have no power and no influence, people who are not important in the eyes of the world. Seek out simple people who have little but who have a simple and sincere faith in God. Try to learn from their example.

Don't do something just because "everyone is doing it." For example, even empirical studies reveal that sex outside of marriage and "living together" before marriage are popular traps that frequently result in unhappy relationships, failed marriages, and great sadness for everyone involved. The traditional Christian prohibition of premarital sex and "living together" came from many centuries of experience. Is it not arrogant and foolish to disregard this traditional wisdom? If you strive to cultivate intimacy with the risen Lord and participate in the life of a good faith community, healthy human friendships will come into your life, and if your calling is to marriage you will find the spouse best for you.

CHAPTER 9

On Accepting the Will of God

Sometimes we pray, "Lord, help me to know your will, and help me to do your will." But keep in mind that there are two wills involved in the will of God—there is your will and God's will, and not infrequently God works with your will. As long as you try to live a prayerful life, and prayerfully read the Scriptures, and use your common sense, and pay attention to what gifts and talents God has given you, then you will not have much difficulty discovering the will of God for you.

Of course, sometimes the will of God comes to us in events and experiences we don't find to be pleasant or enjoyable. God gets involved with accidents, too, you know. If you break an arm, or you become unemployed, or a loved one dies, or you learn that you yourself are going to die from a terminal illness—God is there, God's love is part of what's going on for you now. The will of God, our loving father, is for you to be open to his infinite love in this situation, and as you work with it he will work with it, too. As Saint Paul says, "We know that all things work together for good for those who love God…" (Romans 8:28). You can count on it.

CHAPTER 10

On Not Letting Your Tongue
Run Away With You

We are created by God, our loving father, to live together with other people, and work together, and be there for one another. But sometimes we have an inclination to talk too much, and that's a fact—especially about empty-headed nonsense. Yes, it's good to be with friends and talk about seemingly inconsequential matters; that's one of the ways we share ourselves with one another. But there needs to be limits. You need time to be with family alone, and you need time, at least now and then, for prayerful solitude. Balance, that is the key.

Even conversations that focus on significant topics can get out of hand. There comes a point, even in the most important spiritual conversation, when any more talking will do more harm than good. Cultivate the ability to know when enough is enough, take a "to be continued" approach, and excuse yourself.

CHAPTER 11

Finding Peace and Learning to Want Spiritual Maturity

Considerable peace of mind and heart could be ours if we weren't so concerned with the opinions and behavior of other people. How can we possibly be at peace if we constantly concern ourselves with what is none of our business, if we constantly seek to escape through mere "entertainment," or worse through some form of substance abuse? How can we be truly at peace if we almost never place ourselves calmly in the presence of God? Happiest are those who make regular times to be quietly alone with God, for they will have true peace of mind and heart.

How do you think many of the saints, both ancient and modern, learned to be truly prayerful people? They chose to practice freedom from compulsions, they asked God to help free them from addictions, and they practiced moderation in all things except love for God and neighbor, upon which they placed no limits. This meant that they were free to rely completely upon God even in the most practical, everyday matters. They cultivated intimacy with the Lord Jesus and made this intimacy the center of their lives, day in and day out. The trouble is that our faith—meaning our ongoing relationship with God—rarely goes beyond our intellect; rarely makes a real impact on our everyday lives. We expend almost unlimited energy being anxious and afraid, worrying about all kinds of things, especially the future—over which we have no control whatsoever. Even when we look back and see the countless times when God's love has been there helping us in all kinds of situations we were fearful about, still we find it difficult to trust God here and now.

If we were truly centered on others rather than ourselves, and our hearts were free from addictions—especially addiction to self— then we might be able to feel closer to God and feel his love more present in our hearts. Our biggest problem is a self-centeredness that keeps us from truly giving ourselves in service to God and neighbor. Also, we don't make much effort to follow the inspiration of the saints. Whenever we get a little discouraged or begin to feel stressed out, we are inclined to give up or give in. We turn for comfort to everything but the love of God, including food and television and all kinds of other distractions. Some even turn to pornography and/or substance abuse.

If we resolve to seek out, instead, interests, activities, and forms of recreation that are healthy and that bring true joy, then we will experience the protection and assistance of God, who stands ready to help those who help themselves and place their trust in him. Indeed, there is a sense in which God allows us to make wrong choices, but he wants us to make the right choices so that we might become spiritually healthier and more mature. If we do this, we will find peace of mind and heart and greater intimacy with God.

We have a tendency to put up with ourselves as we are: faults, weaknesses, addictions, and our virtues and talents all rolled into one. Each of us is a mixture of strengths and weaknesses, virtues and vices, as it were, and the older we get the more likely we are to give up trying to become better persons. Instead, growing in our love for God and neighbor should be a lifelong occupation.

Hard Times
Can Have Positive Effects

More often than we might want to admit, when our lives become most difficult we also experience the most growth as spiritual and human beings. For difficulties and hard times, no matter what forms they take, are an opportunity to reach more deeply within ourselves, where our loving God dwells, and to rely more on him today than we did yesterday. Sometimes it's good for us to experience opposition from others, and to be disliked or even despised by others unfairly, even though we have all the best intentions and we're trying to do our best. Such times give us opportunities to become more humble, that is, more aware of the truth about ourselves, both the positive and the negative. When other people treat us unfairly, or ridicule us behind our backs, or tell lies about us, these are opportunities to turn to God, who knows the truth, and ask him to worry about it so we don't need to.

This is why we need to be firmly rooted in God, so that we will have no need to rely upon human approval or encouragement. When we have good intentions but find ourselves stressed out, or tempted to do what we know we should not, or thinking bad thoughts about other people, then we begin to understand our overwhelming need for God's love, for without him we are helpless in this world. When we must put up with such difficulties, the best thing we can do is turn to God in prayer asking for a renewal of hope and patience. Such experiences remind us that in this world we will never have perfect peace and security.

CHAPTER 13

How to Make Good Choices

To be alive is a great good and a tremendous blessing. But all the same, we will never be without difficulties and temptations to do what is not good for us in the long run. As the First Letter of Peter remarks, "Discipline yourselves, keep alert. Like a roaring lion your adversary the devil prowls around, looking for someone to devour" (5:8). Everyone needs to take seriously the need to resist the inclination to engage in behaviors or activities that seem desirable but are actually self-destructive spiritually, emotionally, physically, or all three.

Although these self-destructive tendencies and temptations may be a big hassle and a pain in the neck, they actually serve a good purpose, because by means of them we can grow in humility and become more free and more mature. Even the greatest saints, both ancient and modern, had to struggle with self-destructive inclinations and grew closer to God because of such struggles. There is no place we can go where we will not have to struggle with self-destructive tendencies. Such is the human condition.

The point is that we will never be entirely free from self-destructive inclinations, no matter how many years we live, because we have deep within us a basic self-destructive "shadow self." This is the meaning of the Christian belief in original sin and our "fallen" or flawed condition. Ultimately, we are saved and redeemed by the life, death, and resurrection of Christ, and even now we experience this. But, in the short run, we still live with the effects of our flawed human nature, and we still need to struggle with this.

It's critical to understand that it never works to try to run away from the temptation or to give in to a self-destructive choice. Running away never helps. The only tactic that works is to patiently and prayerfully stand up to each inclination or temptation to self-destructiveness. This is the only way to become strong against self-destructiveness.

The one who continues to tolerate inclinations to engage in self-destructive behaviors instead of renouncing them entirely makes no personal progress. The more we allow any room at all in our lives for self-destructive behaviors, the stronger these tendencies will grow and the sooner they will return full strength to make us miserable. With patient persistence, rather than frantically running away, and with the help of God, a little at a time, you will master your self-destructive inclinations. When you do feel tempted to engage in self-destructive behaviors, and behaviors that harm your relationships with others and with God, find someone with whom you can talk about it. And when someone else is similarly tempted, be kind to him or her and offer comfort and encouragement. Give others the same understanding and kindness you would like to receive yourself.

When the idea first occurs to us to engage in some form of self-destructive behavior, or in some behavior that will hurt others or deprive them of their rights, or to not do what we know is right because we fear the disapproval of others, it's important to not give that idea a chance to get a foothold. Rather, it's important to resist immediately. The slower we are to resist, the more we are likely to give in and the stronger the negative tendency becomes. First comes the simple idea, then the imagination makes the idea seem desirable, then the idea begins to look very attractive, and finally we give in. Then later we regret what we did. But if we resist when the self-destructive idea first pops into our head, then we don't give the idea a chance. That's the way to handle what is traditionally called "temptation to sin."

Some people never find themselves faced by major challenges to their faith, that is, their personal relationship with the risen Christ and with his people, the Church. But then their faith collapses in the face of ordinary, everyday challenges. You can learn a lesson from such experiences, however. Failures can help you grow in the humility you need to never rely only on yourself when it comes to living your faith.

On Not Jumping to Conclusions

It's easy to draw hasty conclusions when observing the words and actions of others. But you really don't know why they act the way they do. You know little if anything about someone else's personal history.

Our opinions of others usually reflect our personal likes and dislikes, and these opinions are usually mistaken because they merely express our personal inclinations. If loving intimacy with God were our only real desire, then we would not become unhappy when everyone doesn't agree with us.

Often our thoughts and actions come not from love for God and neighbor but from some unconscious motive or some influence outside of us of which we're hardly aware. Many people have only their own selfish interests at heart, but they're not aware of that fact. They get along fine with others as long as everything goes their way, but as soon as something happens that they don't like, they lose their peace of mind and become sad or depressed. Often a difference of opinion or a disagreement is what causes friends to abandon one another, even among people who claim to want nothing more than to be good disciples of Christ.

Bad habits we have had for many years are difficult to change, and no one wants to change when he or she is unsure of what the consequences will be. If you think you can reason your way to personal improvement using simple logic or common sense, you're probably wrong. Actually, the only way to leave bad habits behind is to rely on the powerful presence of the risen Christ. There is nothing unreasonable or irrational about authentic Christian faith. God wants us to trust in him completely, even when we're not sure what the consequences will be.

CHAPTER 15

Do Good
With a Loving Heart

Never do something bad even if you think you're doing it out of love or friendship. Also, never underestimate the value of small efforts done with care and compassion. What matters is the intention behind what you do, not how much you do. You do a great deal if whatever you do is done with charitable love and compassion.

You will accomplish a great deal if you do your best at whatever you do, no matter how humble the task. The important thing is to serve others rather than yourself. Sometimes when people look like they are being generous and unselfish, all they are doing is what they are naturally inclined to do, and the real motive is selfish with the hope of gaining some reward.

The one who is truly caring and compassionate toward others has no desire for personal gain. Rather, all he or she wants is to draw attention to the love of God. A person who is really caring and compassionate wants to find happiness only in serving God and neighbor, not in any form of personal profit. Even when such a person sees good in others, he or she recognizes that all goodness is from God.

If we have true caring and compassion toward others, we will recognize that all created things are reminders and reflections of God's infinite goodness and love. At the same time, ultimately we leave all of creation behind to be united eternally with God, so it's important to keep in mind that nothing in creation is an end in itself but rather a reflection and reminder of God's unconditional love for us.

CHAPTER 16

Putting Up With
One Another's Faults and Failings

Just about everyone dislikes something about themselves, and just about everyone dislikes something about other people, too. Often, we can't do anything about what we dislike in ourselves or others, so all we can do is live with what we dislike. The advantage to doing this is that we learn patience, which is difficult but good to learn. While you put up with what you dislike in yourself and others, ask God to help you tolerate what you dislike without whining about it.

Say you notice a fault or weakness in someone else, and it really is your place to try to correct him or her, but you try a couple of times to do this and nothing changes. Don't continue to nag him or her. Instead, turn it over to God and ask that his will be done in this situation. For only God knows how to get something good out of something that irritates you. Faith requires us to learn to bear with one another with patience and kindness. Difficulties in relationships with others reveal the kind of person you really are.

CHAPTER 17

On Living at Peace With Others

If you want to live peacefully with others, there is no getting around the fact that quite often you will need to let others have their way instead of insisting on having your own way. Whether you are married, live in a family, a home you share with others, or a monastery or religious congregation, it's no small matter to do so peacefully. Conflict happens, there's no escaping it. The key is to learn to deal with conflict in ways that nourish rather than disrupt relationships.

One of the best ways to keep your spiritual and emotional equilibrium while living with others is to remind yourself regularly that life is short—you never know how short—and you only get one chance at it, so it's best to do your best at living with others today. For today is all you ever really have.

A daily rededication of yourself to a life of faith, hope, and charitable love for others is all that really matters. Such a life is all that really matters. The one who seeks in a Christian life anything more than a constant struggle for loving intimacy with God and neighbor is in for a big letdown. The only way to have lasting peace is to think of yourself as the least important person and one who is here to be of service to others.

Life comes with plenty of difficulties, hard times, and even suffering, so don't think you can escape any of that. The only way you can get along peacefully and with joy is to be patient, forgiving, and prayerful.

CHAPTER 18

The Examples of Those
Who Have Gone Before You

Pay attention to the example of married couples who have been together for many years and parents whose children are older than your children. Or if you are in a religious order or congregation, watch closely those who have been there far longer than yourself. Seek out the advice of those with more experience in life and those with more Christian faith than you have. Notice all the trials and tribulations they have had to endure, and let their example help give you patience and teach you abandonment to the will of God.

Veteran married couples and parents have had to experience a great many hard times and anguish, yet they remained faithful to each other and did the best they could with their children. Those who have lived many years in religious communities have had more hard times than you can imagine. Of course, there are some few who seem to have had a smooth path through life—but little do you really know, so don't be so sure. The point is that these married couples, parents, and vowed religious have been faithful through many long years, faithful to their vows and faithful to Christ. Learn from them.

These people gave their Christian faith and their marriage or religious vows first place in their lives. Self-forgetfulness was basic to their lives. Husbands and wives made time, without fail, to be with each other; vowed religious made time every day to be with God in prayer and meditation. Married couples preferred a healthy marriage to the accumulation of material possessions. Single people gave generously of their time and resources. Vowed religious had no desire for material comforts but desired only to live in community and serve the people of God.

How easy we found it to be fervent about our marriage or religious vows when we first began! How devoted we were. With time, however, we grew lax, took our spouse for granted or became lukewarm about living a fervent and prayerful religious life in community. Now is the time to rededicate ourselves to the ideals we first vowed to live for a lifetime.

How lukewarm we are about our commitments and how frequently we take our vows for granted. How soon we leave behind our first enthusiasm for marriage, priesthood, single life, or vowed religious life. Rekindle the fire of your first love!

CHAPTER 19

How to Cultivate a Healthy Marriage or Vowed Religious Life

If you want to have a marriage or vowed religious life that will be healthy and happy for fifty or sixty years—and how quickly the years fly by!—you must take practical steps rather than relying on mere fantasies. Whether we are married or living a vowed religious life, we must cultivate our Christian faith every day and attend to our marriage or religious vows regularly.

If you are married, each day remember to tell each other, "I love you dearly." If you are a vowed religious, do not ignore the special place formal prayer times must have in every day's activities. No matter what your fundamental vocation in life, recall several times each day, as Saint Augustine of Hippo said in his *Confessions*, that God is closer to you than you are to yourself. Remember God's loving presence and talk with him often. Don't let prayer become just a once-a-week-on-Sunday thing for you. All of us should pray, "God, help me to maintain my sacred vows and my dedication to you. Give me the grace to begin again each day what I began when I freely took my sacred vows, for all I ever have is the present moment to be faithful to my vows and to you."

If you are going to remain faithful to your sacred commitments, you must resolve firmly each day to put your time where you say your priorities are. If you are married and say that your marriage and family is your top priority, you must make time each day to be with your spouse in ways that nourish your marriage. Physical intimacy between spouses is important and is an experience of the Divine. You must also set aside time each day to be with your children in ways that are good for them. If you are a vowed religious and say that your religious vows are the center of your life, you must make plenty of time each day for prayer and meditation and not make the silly common mistake of thinking that "my work is my prayer." Of course, we can follow through on such commitments only with the grace of God, so we must at all times place our trust in him.

Sometimes it is necessary for good reasons not to fulfill your obligations to your spouse and family or to your prayer commitments within religious life. But don't let such exceptions become a habit. Don't give in to the inclination to spiritual laziness which can take over your life so easily if you allow it. Be aware of how you are thinking about your most basic life commitments, and be aware of what you are actually doing with your time each day, for both have much to do with who you really are as compared to who you think you are.

Find a way to be able to give a few minutes at the beginning and at the end of your day to become consciously aware that you are in the presence of God and that you live in him and he lives in you. Just be aware of this great mystery of love, even if only for a moment. In the morning, ask the Lord Jesus to help you to carry his Holy Spirit into all that you will do and say that day. At night, think back over your day to see how well you accomplished this goal, then thank God for your successes and ask forgiveness for your failures.

No matter what your vocation—to marriage, single life, priesthood, or a vowed religious life—you need to experiment with various kinds of prayer and ways of praying to find what fits your life best. Some people find that the only way they can really pray is by reading prayers from a book, and there is nothing inferior about this at all. Saints such as the great sixteenth-century Carmelite nun and mystic Saint Teresa of Ávila rated such prayer highly. Others may find that a silent form of meditation works best for them. Many—especially family people who lead active lives—may find that the only way they can pray is "on the run," as they go about their daily activities. The point is not the method of prayer used but the praying. A Christian life is a prayerful life regardless of the method of prayer used.

The great holy seasons and days of the liturgical calendar, such as Lent and Easter, Advent and Christmas, should be celebrated in ways that refresh the soul and not merely skimmed through as secular seasons and holidays. Rather, live these weeks and days as the holy times that they are. Allow them to make a real difference in the way you live. If you can, during Advent and Lent participate in Mass every day. If this is impossible, can you go to Mass on one or two days besides Sunday? Never underestimate the power of the Eucharist to make a positive difference in your life.

One of the main purposes of regular prayer is to help us remain spiritually alert. With regular prayer we become sensitive to God's presence in our ordinary everyday activities and receptive to the Word of God in all kinds of everyday ways.

Silence and Solitude Is Important for Everyone

No matter what your vocation, there should be appropriate times for you to enter into silence and solitude. Modern western cultures tend to alienate us from God, from one another, and from ourselves to the point that we can lose much of our inner freedom. In silence and solitude we can recharge our spiritual batteries, so to speak. We can get back in touch with God and with our deepest self. This helps us to act in ways that are more faithful to our Christian calling to be with and love both God and neighbor.

We need to be on guard against the modern tendency to "run with the herd" and allow our lives to be dominated by peer pressure, mere fashion, or what happens to be popular. Sometimes our Christian calling leads us to act in ways contrary to what's "in" or what's promoted by the mass media. Sometimes our Christian calling invites us to resist particular cultural, political, or economic trends. In truth, to be a Christian is to be called to live "in but not of" the dominant popular culture insofar as it is contrary to the gospel. It is only regular times of prayerful silence and solitude that give us the spiritual courage to live in such a manner.

In prayerful silence and solitude we find ourselves face to face with ourselves and with God. This experience helps us to be honest with ourselves and with God so that we can return to our regular lives with a renewed dedication to our highest ideals and goals. In prayerful silence and solitude, we can free ourselves from "running with the herd" for the sake of being "popular" or acceptable to the dominant popular culture.

In prayerful silence and solitude we can renew our trust in God and free ourselves from over-reliance on ourselves and our own efforts. We can regain some perspective on our normal, everyday preoccupations. We can "let go and let God."

You may think you are too busy to make time for prayerful

silence and solitude, but it is precisely the one who is too busy who needs silence and solitude the most. Even the busiest person can find a way to make time for the occasional day away from the usual activities and preoccupations for some time in prayerful silence and solitude. Spouses and parents can give each other a day away now and then. They need to do this, at the very least, for the sake of their marriage and for the sake of their children. The busiest business-person, even for the sake of his or her business, needs to take a day—at least every month or two—for prayerful silence and solitude. If you want to experience firsthand the healing presence of God in your heart, you must seek out regular times of prayerful silence and solitude. In silence and solitude you will refresh yourself and regain your spiritual balance so you can return to your regular activities with your head screwed on straight again.

Don't be frightened or anxious at the prospect of silence and solitude. There is nothing to it. Keep it simple. You will find great spiritual refreshment by sitting quietly with the Scriptures open before you. Read slowly through the psalms or one of the gospels, pausing when a line or phrase touches your heart. Then simply speak to God from your heart; say whatever is on your mind.

Once you get into the habit of setting aside a day every month or two for prayerful silence and solitude, you will find that you can't wait to get back to it the next time. You may find yourself thinking that it's selfish to want this time of silence and solitude. What nonsense. These times away are as much for the sake of others and the sake of your work as they are for your own sake. You can't give what you don't have. Your business or job will suffer if you don't have these times of prayerful silence and solitude. You will become a stressed-out, difficult-to-work-with person if you don't have these times of silence and solitude. You could even become physically ill if you don't have your regular times of prayerful silence and solitude.

Don't kid yourself. Regular times of prayerful silence and solitude are necessary for practical reasons as much as for spiritual ones! The bottom line is this: there is no greater source of healing, peace, and rejuvenation than times of prayerful silence and solitude with

God, our loving father, with his Son, and with their Holy Spirit. There is no greater source of liberation from all that drags us down. There is no better way to fill your heart with all that you need to love God and neighbor.

CHAPTER 21

Readiness To Be
Transformed in Christ's Love

If you want to have a rich, meaningful, purposeful life, become more aware of how great is God's love for you, for all people, and for all of creation. Do not be frivolous, but do allow the joy that comes from true faith and hope to be more present in your everyday life. Be intentional about welcoming transformation in Christ, and you will find yourself living a balanced life of faith, hope, and loving charity. Don't be afraid to face up to your faults and failings, and resolve to overcome them with God's grace. There is no doubt that you will find happiness in this life if you remember that life is short and that sometimes—although not always—the values of the dominant popular culture are as phony as can be. Remember that your ultimate destiny is not in this world and that you were created to be eternally united with God.

How happy you will be if you can turn away from the distractions of empty forms of entertainment and dissipation and become aware of your loving intimacy with God's love and forgiveness. How blessed you will be if you turn away from diversions that do little more than weigh down your heart. Be courageous, for only good habits will help you to break bad habits. If you leave other people alone when they are involved in empty diversions, then they will leave you alone to occupy yourself with healthy, meaningful occupations.

In a culture that values comfort, convenience and financial security above all else, don't be too interested in any of these things. Just go about your business doing the best you can and let everything else take care of itself in God's own good time. If you give a few minutes each day to being prayerfully aware of God's love in and all around you, then you will have all that you need when you need it.

Never forget that God brought you into existence out of his infinite love, a love that will never end. You can reject God's love and forgiveness, but God will never turn his back on you. No one has a life free from troubles, but never think that because you have hard times God has forgotten you. Nothing could be further from the truth. Even outright suffering and death itself are but reminders to rely more upon God's love, which is always trustworthy. If you are sorry for your sins—that is, for the ways you have freely chosen to harm yourself and your relationships with God, other people, and the earth our home—and try to do what you can to make up for the harm you have done, that is all that God needs in order to forgive you.

Reflect sometimes on the fact of your own mortality. You have a limited number of years, days, and hours in this life, and your main concern should always be to love God and neighbor. That is the purpose of your existence. If you recall, now and then, that one day you will die, that will help you to keep your priorities straight. This will help you to remember what's really important in this life and what's not important at all.

The last thing a consumer culture wants us to remember is that life is short and that no amount of escapist diversions can change that fact. Remember that even the most affluent of lifestyles will never satisfy the hunger of the human heart. Only by entering into loving intimacy with God and other people and by trying to live a life that is healthy and free from addictions to harmful substances can one find real meaning and purpose in life.

Reflection on the Human Condition

No matter where you are or what you are doing, you are going to have a life of frustration and dissatisfaction unless you open your heart to loving intimacy with God, which naturally should manifest itself in love of one's neighbor.

It makes no sense to be unhappy when things don't go the way you want them to go. Who ever gets everything he or she wants? Nobody, that's who. Not a person on this earth is without some hardship, difficulty, or suffering, not even the wealthiest person in the world, not even the most powerful person in the world, and not even the most prominent religious leader. Who is the most content with life? Only the one who is ready and willing to put up with life's trials and troubles with a patient, loving heart and with trust in God.

How unhappy people are who have an overabundance of this world's wealth and comfort but have no concern for those who suffer injustice and poverty. They will soon learn, to their sorrow, that the things they cherish so much have no power to give them lasting peace of mind and heart.

Truly happy people, including all the saints and all those who put love of God and neighbor first in their lives, constantly strive to live a simple life and share what they have with those who have little. Their main care in life is to give themselves to the love of God and neighbor.

Whatever you do, don't put off your decision to become a true person of faith, hope, and charitable love. It is when you feel most troubled and anxious that you can best make this choice. Don't wait for a time when your life is trouble-free and you have no fears or anxieties because such a time will never come. Faith and hope make the most sense when you need them the most, so begin today.

Consider Your Own Mortality

Life is short. No matter how young you are now, the day is not far off when you will be surprised by how old you have become. It's true! Sometimes it looks like only insurance sales people believe that you will ever grow old and die. As Christians, we believe in life eternal after death, a life lived in the joyful mystery of the resurrection of Christ. But that does not mean that death is somehow meaningless or doesn't really happen. On the contrary, as Buddhism teaches—and Christianity has always taught, even if many Christians overlook it in our time—we can only live a good life if we take to heart our own mortality.

How often we hear that this person or that person died suddenly, with no warning whatsoever, "cut down in the prime of life." The truth is that we never know how long we will live. Relatively young people die suddenly every day. "It's a mighty world we live in, but the truth is we're only passin' through," wrote John R. Cash and Randy Scruggs in their song "Passin' Through."

How long do you think you'll be remembered after you die? Will there be anyone to pray for you once you are gone? My friend, the present is all you have, so do the best you can with it, for you don't know when you will die. While you live, try to make love for God, loving charity toward others, and kindness to the earth your most basic concern. Maintain good relationships with others in this world, but cultivate friendships, too, with good men and women—including saints, ancient and modern—who have already passed over to the next life.

Remember that you're "only passin' through," so don't live as if you're going to live in this world forever. Your concern for his world's cares and worries should not consume your heart, but keep your heart open to God's love. Each day take a moment to be aware of God's love in and all around you, and ask him to welcome you into eternity after you die. Amen.

The Merciful Love of God

Sometimes you may think that you are a great sinner, indeed. However, don't flatter yourself! Nothing you have ever done, and nothing you will ever do, is beyond the mercy of God. The instant you are truly sorry for sins great or small and declare yourself ready to mend your ways, God, your loving father, is more than ready to forgive you and welcome you as if you had never been away.

Consider the story of the Prodigal Son in the Gospel of Luke. The son sins by going off to blow all the money he got from his father when he demanded his inheritance. Then, of course, the son runs smack into the harsh, cruel world, has second thoughts, and decides to return home.

> "So he set off and went to his father. But while he was still far off, his father saw him and was filled with compassion; he ran and put his arms around him and kissed him. Then the son said to him, 'Father, I have sinned against heaven and before you; I am no longer worthy to be called your son.' But the father said to his slaves, 'Quickly, bring out a robe—the best one—and put it on him; put a ring on his finger and sandals on his feet. And get the fatted calf and kill it, and let us eat and celebrate; for this son of mine was dead and is alive again; he was lost and is found!' And they began to celebrate" (Luke 15:20–24).

Notice that the father is "filled with compassion" and runs to embrace and kiss his son even before the wayward son says anything about being sorry. And notice that the father doesn't lecture the son, or even reply directly to his expression of repentance. He is too busy celebrating his son's return to think about lectures or punishment. This is an excellent illustration of the attitude that God, our loving father, has toward us. Even before we say we're sorry, we're forgiven. Consider the words of the great theologian Paul Tillich about the meaning of salvation: "Accept yourself as accepted in spite of being unacceptable."

We find it so difficult sometimes to believe in a God who is merciful. But the fact is that God's love for us is absolutely reliable. In response to and embraced by that love, we repent of our sin.

CHAPTER 25

Being Sincere About
Turning Your Life Around

Faithfulness is what a Christian life requires, not perfection. When Jesus calls us to be perfect (see Matthew 5:48 and 19:21), his point is to encourage us to be indiscriminate when it comes to charitable love. Jesus doesn't demand some impossible human perfection.

Remember that your baptism set you on a path that requires in all things a constant love for God and neighbor. Remain faithful and constant in doing good for God, for others, and for the earth. Never give up hope, and don't get cocky when your efforts seem to be a big success. If you do that, you may become overconfident and start to backslide.

There was once a man who worried a lot about whether he was "saved" or not. Fundamentalist Christians told him that all he had to do was "accept Jesus Christ as your personal savior" and he would instantly be "saved." Catholics and others told him that "salvation is a lifelong process that depends on constant trust in God." One day the man was bummed out and depressed, worrying about this, so he went into a church to pray. He kept thinking, *If only I could be certain that I will remain constant in my faith until the end of my life.* Then he "heard" a voice in his mind that said, *If you did know that you would remain constant until the end, how would that affect your life? What would you do? Well, whatever you would do, go ahead and do that. If you do that, then all shall be well.* The man took comfort from this thought. He gave himself entirely to God's will and made a habit of doing so at the beginning of every day. He no longer worried about his eternal destiny. He was no longer concerned about what his future would be. Instead, he wanted only to know God's will and delight whenever he made a decision or choice and whenever he wanted to do good for others. This man learned that the only thing worth doing in this life is to love God and act out of charitable love for others.

Recall often that you are a baptized Christian living in the risen Christ. Your primary calling is to let him transform your life and to become his presence in your little corner of the world. The joyful disciple of Christ who reflects often on the life, death, and resurrection of our Lord will find everything he or she needs to live a life that is worthwhile. Each morning, open your heart to the risen Christ, and if you do this you will have a life with meaning and purpose. Remember your baptism.

The sincere and prayerful Christian finds God's will in all the ordinary events of every day—both the pleasant and the unpleasant. The lukewarm or insincere Christian finds life to be one hassle after another and experiences anxiety and anguish time after time. Such a person does not have the spiritual resources to see God's will in all things and so has no source of comfort and consolation, no source of light in the midst of darkness. Therefore, he or she is wide open to disaster. The one who only seeks an easy life will always be in trouble of one kind or another.

Perhaps you think you have a difficult life. But think of the millions of people in the world who live in hunger and poverty with little more than the shabby clothes on their backs to call their own. Think of the countless people who are homeless, even in your own country. Think of the many more in other parts of the world who don't even have a roof over their heads. Yet many of these people have a faith in God that puts your faith to shame. Self-pity is a luxury such people cannot afford. Remember the vast number of God's children who have it so much worse than you do, and stop whining. Get over it, and praise God for the many blessings you take for granted most of the time!

When you get to the point where you can see the Divine Presence in all people and all of creation—and even in yourself—then you will know what it is to taste God, and you will be satisfied with whatever you have. Then you won't be thrilled to have too much nor depressed when you have too little. Rather, you will rest confidently in the risen Christ who "is all and in all!" (Colossians 3:11).

Keep your eyes on the goal you have set before you to live your life according to the gospel of Jesus Christ. Remember that all you ever have is the present moment and that, once that moment is gone, it will never return. If you allow yourself to become spiritually lazy, you will become spiritually ill. If you open yourself to the presence of the risen Lord every day, however, you will find a peace you can never lose, and your daily work on behalf of others will be a light burden, indeed. All this will be the result of God's life in you and the sincerity of your faith.

Above all, thank the risen Christ for his grace and companionship. True faith does not mean you will never have doubts and questions and days when discouragement may seem about to win out. But with the support of God, you will be ready to face anything that comes your way. Faith—meaning intimacy with God—can be hard work at times, just as any worthwhile relationship takes hard work sometimes. If you do all you can, however, and then entrust yourself to our risen Lord, and to the prayers of his Blessed Mother, Mary, you need have no fear. Even in the face of death, you may be sure that all shall be well.

If you do your best each day, thanking God for all his gifts, and humbly asking forgiveness for your sins and failures, then each evening will be enjoyable. Be watchful. Don't allow yourself to ever give up, and always attend to your spiritual life by moments of prayer and regular participation in the liturgies of the Church. Then you need have no concern about either this life or the next. Rejoice always!

BOOK II

On the Interior
Life of the
Follower of Christ

CHAPTER 1

Living From the Inside Out

It is essential to a life of Christian faith to keep everything in perspective. Learn to see the Divine Presence in all things and all places, even the most ordinary events of everyday life. Then, the anxieties and fears that are so common will not bother you as much. Because of your baptism, the peace and courage of the risen Christ are present in your deepest center. It takes an open heart to realize that you already have what you seek. Indeed, the love of God permeates your being, and the risen Christ delights to dwell within you at all times. The Lord Jesus often makes his presence felt to the one who takes the time to be open to him. He will speak silently to you, and give you comfort, encouragement, and a peace that goes beyond understanding.

Make room for Christ in your heart and allow into your spiritual center only what is compatible with his presence. When you realize and accept that Christ is present in you, then you will understand that you need nothing else in this world, because he makes you rich in all that matters. In the long run, you never know who your friends are and who is against you. Upon God alone you can rely absolutely.

Be a good friend to others and, if you are married, be a trusting and trustworthy spouse. Ask the Lord Jesus to be in your friendships and at the center of your marriage so that all may be lasting and healthy. God's love will be there for you in all things and help all things to become what is best for you. Remember that you are on pilgrimage in this life, on your way to your only true home, and here you will find no perfect peace.

You will feel at home in this world only to the extent that you can see God's divine love in creation, in other people, and in your everyday life with both its darkness and its light. Be on the lookout always for God who is just around every corner and behind every leaf, always following you hoping to capture your heart with love.

For all their beauty and goodness, however, don't mistake the things of this world for God. Rather, always see that it is God's love and grace that shines through all things and don't be distracted by surface appearances.

Try to put things in perspective. If you cherish your faith-relationship with the risen Lord, you will have a vibrant and active interior life, and that is where you will live your life—from your heart. No matter what happens, you will be able at any time to turn in complete trust to God, abandon yourself to him, and know that all will be well.

The one who learns to walk in the light of eternity and the light of God's love has a life of faith, hope, and charitable love. Such a person needs no special place or time to engage in religious practices, such as prayer, meditation, and spiritual reading and reflection. He or she makes sure these things happen each day, and they are as likely to happen during a lunch hour or other ordinary time as they are to happen at some especially designated time of silence and solitude.

The person of true faith can gather and focus himself or herself in a few moments, because he or she never allows the self to become completely dissipated or distracted in work or other activities. The center of peace and calm is always there in which to turn.

If your heart and soul were at one with God, everything would be a benefit to you, whether pleasant or unpleasant. If you are often upset and disturbed, that is because you do not yet live continuously in the presence of the risen Christ. You forget him and become disconnected, because you forget that he is always with you—closer than you are to yourself. If you find God lovingly present in all things and all happenings, then you will have a life of peace beyond understanding. Of course, this rarely happens perfectly in this world for us ordinary followers of Christ, but you can always return to an awareness of God's presence in and all around you at any time.

CHAPTER 2

Being One With
God's Will in All Things

Don't worry about who is for you and who is against you, because it doesn't matter at all. All that matters is that God is always for you at all times and in all places. If you begin each day with prayer, offering your day to God, and end your day with prayer, asking his forgiveness and thanking him for all his blessings, then all shall be well. When unpleasant or bad things happen to you and you take it without complaining or whining, you will, without a doubt, experience God's support and assistance. Even though you find it difficult to believe sometimes, God truly wants to help you and save you from your troubles. Don't get in a funk if others know about your weaknesses and failures, because they help you to not get an inflated sense of yourself.

The idea is not to "let people walk all over you," but to simply be who and what you are—no more, no less. That's true humility. The truly humble person neither brags nor grovels. Such a person is close to God because the simple truth is all that God cares about. Therefore, that is all that you should care about, too.

CHAPTER 3

The Person Who Loves Peace

If you have peace in your own heart, then you will be able to bring peace to others. In fact, the person of peace can do more good in this world than anyone else, regardless of his or her level of education. Those who act without thinking, and without a true desire for peace, turn good into evil, and they are always ready to attribute evil motives to others. The person who is good and loves peace, however, turns everything into good.

If you live in peace, you will believe evil of no one. Those who are constantly dissatisfied and complaining are suspicious all the time; they have no peace, and they don't want others to have peace, either. They often say what they should not and rarely say what they should. They have no difficulty remembering what others should do, but they easily forget their own responsibilities. Therefore, pay attention to your own obligations. Do first what you would rather not do, and only then do what you enjoy doing. Don't give a thought to what others are supposed to do unless you are obliged to do so as part of your responsibilities—and then do so tactfully. Correct others with kindness and patience.

You're slick when it comes to making excuses for your own failures and hiding your mistakes; therefore, be just as patient when it comes to listening to the excuses of others. You should find it easier to accept the excuses of others than to accept your own excuses. If you want others to tolerate you, you must learn to tolerate them. Of course, there are some people and situations that are, frankly, clinically dysfunctional, and you should get away from those as soon as you can.

Peace in this world comes only when we quietly tolerate ordinary, everyday injustices we might assume are purposely aimed at us instead of doing everything we can to avoid such irritations. The person who can let such experiences not touch his or her deepest center of peace is the happiest person in this world. The one who can do this is the friend of Christ and gains a taste of the peace of heaven—even in this life.

CHAPTER 4

Having a Pure and Simple Heart and a Sincere Purpose

You can find spiritual freedom by developing two virtues: simplicity and a pure heart. "Simplicity" refers to keeping one purpose uppermost in mind: the love of God and neighbor. As long as this is your single most important purpose in life, you will be free from any obstacles to this purpose, because everything else will serve or facilitate that purpose. Anything that gets in the way of love for God and charitable love for others must have no place in your life. Purity of heart is essentially the same thing. The pure of heart have but one goal in life against which everything else is measured: to love God and neighbor. Simplicity and purity of heart make it possible to integrate your life around the ultimate purpose of life: to love God and neighbor. No matter what else finds a place in your life, including your fundamental life vocation (marriage, single life, vowed religious life, priesthood), your work, and your hobbies and recreation, as long as your choices contribute to your primary dedication to love of God and neighbor, you will be a person of peace and joy.

Just as a computer's clean-up and defragmenting programs keep it functioning efficiently, so you lose your spiritual laziness when you have simplicity and purity of heart, and you become like a new person. Just as a computer's anti-virus software keeps it functioning at its peak, so you will know peace and spiritual vigor when you delete anything from your life that gets in the way of your love for God and neighbor.

The Need To Be
Vigilant About Yourself

It's a good idea to guard against becoming overconfident, because it's so easy for us to act out of ignorance and selfishness. It's so easy for us to be blind to what really matters in life, and often we are completely unaware of our blindness. For example, sometimes we act foolishly and then compound our foolishness by making excuses for ourselves. Likewise, we criticize others for their little mistakes or flaws while completely ignoring our own major defects. Or we are quick to notice when others criticize or embarrass us, but we pay no attention to the ways we hurt or embarrass others. If you accurately evaluate yourself, you won't be nearly as quick to judge and condemn others.

You will deepen your faith and intimacy with Christ if you stop worrying about what might happen to you in the future and just do the best you can here and now. Let nothing be important to you except love for God and neighbor and the gifts that come from God alone. If you love God and neighbor, everything else will seem less important, and you will recognize that any joy and peace you know comes from God alone.

CHAPTER 6

On the Joy of Knowing
You're Doing OK

In the old Disney animated movie version of *Pinocchio*, the little wooden puppet has no conscience, so the Blue Fairy gives him one in the form of a conscientious cricket named Jiminy Cricket. It's Jiminy Cricket's job to tell Pinocchio what's right and what's wrong, but Pinocchio is still free either to heed or to ignore Jiminy Cricket's guidance. This gives us a cute image of what we mean by "conscience," but unfortunately it's not an accurate one. Conscience is not a little voice that automatically tells us what's right and what's wrong. Conscience is the human faculty that must be formed and educated to help us distinguish between right and wrong behaviors and choices. Conscience can be properly informed or misinformed. Assuming that your conscience is well and accurately informed, if you have "a good conscience," that is, one that approves of how your life is going, you will always have a quiet joy that will not abandon you.

People who habitually make bad or unhealthy choices and engage in bad or unhealthy behaviors are never happy people. No matter how pleasant and comfortable their lives seem, their bad and unhealthy choices and behaviors are guaranteed to lead to unhappiness. True joy comes from a clear conscience and from knowing that you are accepted by a loving God in spite of being unacceptable if left to your own devices. True joy comes from knowing that you possess the truth, and the truth is not merely what feels good to you but what a well-formed and well-informed conscience tells you is good. This is why you will have joy as long as you care nothing for either praise or blame from other people, but only for the approval of a Christian conscience.

What does it mean to have a good conscience and a pure heart? It means to be inwardly disposed toward God at all times so that you are never controlled by anything but the requirements of the love of God and neighbor.

On Cherishing the Companionship
of Christ Above All Else

Happy and blessed is the person who understands what it means to cherish the companionship of the risen Christ and to seek the guidance of the Holy Spirit in all things. Happy and blessed is the one who relies on the sacraments of the Church and the Church's liturgy for the support and nourishment to be found there always. Imperfect and sometimes even sinful as the Church's members are, the Church is also holy and provides us with the sacraments of Christ that are so fundamental to our spiritual well-being.

The risen Lord wants to be your completely trustworthy companion and guide in all things. Therefore, listen to all other companions and guides only insofar as they agree or are compatible with the Lord Jesus. If you listen to advice from other sources and know that it conflicts with the guidance of the risen Christ, you may be sure that you'll end up miserable and frustrated.

Love the Lord Jesus and make him your most important friend and companion. When all other friends and companions abandon you, he will be there for you and will keep you safe. Like it or not, the day will come when you will be separated from friends and all the things in this world that gave you comfort. Perhaps only then will you truly appreciate the absolutely reliable love and companionship of the Lord Jesus.

One thing you can count on as absolutely reliable: the love of the risen Christ in good times and bad, in life and in death. He alone can be trusted when every other help has abandoned you.

If you can keep everything secondary to Christ, then you will have a firm sense that he is with you at all times. If you put anything else in a more important place in your life than Christ, you will find that you have made a big mistake. If you seek Christ in all things, you will find him. But if you seek only your own self-interest, that is what you will find, but the result will be disastrous. You do yourself

more harm by not seeking Jesus and by not participating in the sacramental, social, and educational life of the Church than if all the
world and a great many enemies were out to hurt you in countless
ways.

Cultivating Friendship
With the Lord Jesus

When you are aware of the presence of the Lord Jesus, everything is
good, and your work seems a light burden, indeed. But when you
are not aware of his presence, life becomes wearisome and difficult.
When we do not listen to the voice of Christ speaking within our
heart, we are unhappy, but when we do listen and trust in him, then
we feel hopeful and energetic.

How lethargic and even depressed you are when you are not
aware of the presence of the risen Christ in and all around you! It's
a big waste of time and energy when you desire anything other than
Christ. To lose a prayerful awareness of his presence is to suffer a
great loss, even greater than if you were to lose life itself.

What, really, can the world offer you that is better than Christ
and better than all that you get from participation in the life of his
community of faith, the Church? The Church and its official repre-
sentatives are far from perfect. Still, to be without Christ and the
Church is a source of pain and anguish, but to be with him and with
his people, the Church, is sweet. If Christ is with you, no lasting
harm can come to you, even in the face of death itself. Whoever
learns to live with Christ has the greatest of treasures, and whoever
loses Christ loses more than all the riches in the world.

It is something of an art to learn how to live with Christ and
with his Church, and to know how to cultivate the friendship of
Christ takes wisdom. It is easy for other things to look more attractive than friendship with the Lord Jesus, and sometimes the sinfulness and ignorance of his people, the Church, can lead to thinking

that the Church isn't all that important. It takes patience, humility, and the ability to forgive to see that, even with all its failings, the Church remains a unique source of divine life. Don't forget that you yourself are sinful and far from perfect; therefore, you need the forgiveness of God's people as much as they need your forgiveness. It is naive to expect the Church, meaning all of us, to be without flaws and failures when you yourself have more than your share of flaws and failures.

If you choose to turn away from Christ and from his people, the Church, and focus your life on worldly things, you will soon find yourself unhappy and frustrated. Where else but in the Church can you find the sacraments by which you nourish your intimacy with the Lord Jesus in ways unavailable anyplace else? Without Christ and his Church you will find it extremely difficult to live your life, and you will be sad and lonely.

Show charitable love for everyone else for the sake of Jesus, and love him for his own sake. In fact, it is only love for Christ that will make it possible for you to love other people faithfully and with forgiveness and patience. For only he can support your heart when others fail to return your love. He alone is perfectly loving and faithful. Only he makes it possible to love with charity people you don't naturally feel inclined to love. Pray that all may come to know him and his love.

Don't expect anyone but Christ to love you perfectly, then you will be able to love others faithfully, even when they fail to love you in return. Only when husband and wife love Christ will they have the emotional and spiritual resources to love each other over a lifetime of marriage. Only Christ makes it possible for a marriage to be all that it can be.

Be inwardly free from captivation by anything except the love of Christ. Then you will have a life that is worth living. When you ask for and freely receive the love of Christ, you will find that you have the resources to do everything you need to do. When, however, you turn away from the love of Christ, you will find yourself weak and listless. You will feel sad and find that your life is without purpose.

Even then, however, do not give in to despair, but patiently call upon God to help you bear patiently whatever difficulties may come your way. Remember that after the winter comes the spring, after the darkest night comes the dawn of a new day, and after the storm comes the greatest calm. So it will be with you, as well, if you entrust yourself completely to the love of God who cares more for you than you could ever care for yourself.

CHAPTER 9

When Love Isn't Easy and Fun

When you feel the loving presence of Christ, it's easy to think that you can accomplish anything. But the ideal is to be able to act rightly and with loving charity toward all, even when you don't feel inclined to do so or when you feel down in the dumps.

There is nothing special about being happy and giving time to prayer and meditation or good works on behalf of others when you feel God's love within your heart. When you are carried along by God's grace like this, you find everything easy, and it would be nice if we felt like this all the time.

Remember, however, that your faith can never become that of an adult as long as you must have comfort and consolation from God in order to act and live as you should. True love means being able to do all that you should and act rightly, even when you don't feel like doing so. True love means acting for the glory of God and the good of others, even when it isn't enjoyable to do so. At such times love must be a sheer act of the will, and that is the purest form of love.

Sure, we like it when we feel happy about praying and when it's easy to care for others with loving charity. But often this is not how we feel, and we still need to do what's right and what we know God wants us to do. One of the great martyrs of the twentieth century is Saint Maximilian Kolbe, whose love inspired him to die in another man's place in Auschwitz, the infamous World War II Nazi death camp. Father Kolbe's love for God and neighbor was greater even than his love for his own life. It certainly was not easy or fun to do what he did, but he did it all the same. You, too, must learn to surrender yourself.

Of course, before we can do this, we have a lifetime, either long or short, in which to practice, as it were, giving ourselves entirely to God without looking anyplace else for support or consolation. The more we deal with hardship and difficulties, and even with outright suffering, without whining, the more we learn to rely on God alone.

It takes someone who is spiritually grown-up to continue praying and serving others, even when you don't feel like it and get no joy from doing so. It's time to grow up!

CHAPTER 10

Be Thankful for All of God's Blessings

Don't plan on ever having a life of ease and relaxation. Rather, there is no human life that is free from anxiety, hard times, and even outright suffering. Therefore, be ready for difficulties rather than for an easy life. Sure, anyone would rather have an easy life, but chances are you will never have a life free from anxiety and hard times.

Even in the midst of hard times, you can have a spiritual joy that goes way beyond anything this world can offer. Worldly pleasures and fun are empty in the long run, whereas spiritual joy and the consolation that comes from God give real meaning to life.

If you get cocky and overconfident, or think you're free to do anything you like with no unpleasant consequences, you have another think coming. This kind of outlook on life is actually an obstacle to receiving the joy and comfort that come only from God. Sure, God is generous when it comes to giving joy and comfort, but you make a big mistake if you don't give all the credit to God when you have good times and happy days. For the bottom line is this: all you have and all you enjoy, even through your own efforts, ultimately comes from God who gave you the talents and capabilities to do what you did. Never forget that.

If you should have hard times, anxiety, or physical or mental suffering, know that God never wills that we have sorrows or difficulties. Still, such experiences can help us to draw closer to God if we embrace and celebrate life and goodness, even in the midst of darkness and difficulties. Always be hopeful, no matter what.

CHAPTER 11

Not Many People Understand the Power of Welcoming the Cross

Many people love the idea of a heavenly kingdom of light and joy, but few understand that in Christian faith we can know the joy of the Resurrection only by way of the anguish and pain of the cross. In baptism we share in both the cross and the Resurrection of Christ. This means that the darkness and anguish we experience is the darkness and anguish of Christ, and the joy and light that we know is the joy and light of Christ. So when we suffer, our suffering is the suffering of Christ, and when we rejoice, our rejoicing is not just our own small joy, but the eternal joy of Christ. Therefore, both our sorrow and our joy have an eternal nature and an eternal meaning, because they are a sharing in the sorrow and joy of Christ the Lord.

Remember, then, that when your life seems dark and stressful, you are sharing in the cross of Jesus. Such suffering is far from meaningless and without purpose. If you accept pain and anxieties when they come and offer them as prayer for the good of others, then they have meaning and purpose. If you recall in times of joy and happiness that these are a sharing in the resurrection of the Lord Jesus, then you will give thanks to him alone.

Of course, it's not often that you meet someone whose relationship with the Lord Jesus is so strong that he or she can give thanks in both good times and bad. When you do meet such a person, therefore, treasure your friendship with him or her and try to learn from that person's good example. Try to learn that in both life and death you are in God's loving care. So really, there is never anything to be worried about. Never.

CHAPTER 12

True Faith Includes the Cross

For some people, Christian faith is supposed to be a warm fuzzy feeling, and "love" is what it's all about. They overlook words of Jesus in the gospels, such as: "If any want to become my followers, let them deny themselves and take up their cross and follow me. For those who want to save their life will lose it, and those who lose their life for my sake will find it" (Matthew 16:24–25).

Don't be afraid of the cross when it comes into your life, for everyone must walk the way of the cross in order to share in the resurrection of Christ. In other words, darkness, anguish, and suffering come to everyone sooner or later, and as Christians we see such difficulties as part of the mystery of salvation. We don't seek anguish and suffering, of course, but when they come into our life we know they have meaning and purpose rather than being meaningless and futile.

Because Jesus went before us carrying his cross, sharing in the depths of human suffering and death, our own hard times, anguish, suffering, and death unite us to him and, in the end, to his resurrection and eternal life. We take comfort in the assurance that Christ will help us to carry our cross. Bear patiently with hard times, anxieties, and suffering, and you will find that your life will go well and you will have peace.

Indeed, no life is without struggle, anxiety, pain, and ultimately suffering and death. But in virtue of your baptism, your cross is the cross of Christ that leads to a share in his resurrection. So do not be discouraged or without hope. For the joy of Christ's resurrection awaits you, even in the midst of hard times, worries, suffering, and death. Thanks be to God!

BOOK III

On Spiritual
Comfort

Christ Speaks in the
Quiet of Your Heart

"Let me hear what God the LORD will speak…" (Psalm 85:8). How happy you will be when the Lord Jesus speaks quietly his comforting words to your innermost heart. How blessed is the one who listens carefully to the quiet whisperings of Christ and disregards the raucous noise of an entertainment-saturated culture. How blessed is the person whose eyes disregard the inane superficialities that fill so much of the popular entertainment media. How blessed is the one who can gaze with joy upon the great beauty of God's creation and see God present there in all that he has made. How blessed you will be when you can see the face of Christ in the sunrise and in the moon in the night sky and in the faces of those around you.

Here is what the creator of the universe says in the inner quiet of your heart: "I am your salvation, your only true peace, and your life. Remember that I live in you at all times and in all places, and you will have peace. Don't waste your time on nonsense or empty distractions but seek instead all things good, true, and beautiful. Once you learn to see me in all of creation and in all people and learn to live for me and for those with whom you live and work most closely—as well as for those who are poor and sad no matter where they live—you will have true happiness."

My soul, my deepest self, learn to see the love of God in all things, and learn to overlook the great foolishness that the popular culture often tries to pawn off on you as real. See and hear only God reflected in all things bright and good and in all people whether they be sad or happy.

CHAPTER 2

Truth Speaks Within Us
Without the Need for Words

The follower of Christ speaks: "Speak, for your servant is listening" (1 Samuel 3:10). "I am your servant; give me understanding, / so that I may know your decrees" (Psalm 119:125).

I don't care so much to hear from any of your prophets, O Lord. Instead, I want you to speak directly to me in the silence of my heart. You have no need for prophets, for you alone can teach me all that I need to know. True, the great prophets of old were able to speak your words, but they could not give your Spirit. Their words are often wise, but if you remain silent, those words do not make our hearts burn with your joy and your courage.

The prophets of old teach your message, but only you can instruct our hearts. They teach your word, but you alone can enable us to understand. They show the way, but only you can give us the courage to walk that path. The words of the prophets stay on the surface of our lives unless you instruct us and enlighten us. They water the soil, but only you can make the seeds grow.

Speak to me, then, Lord God, and give comfort to my heart. Open my heart that I may hear your words and let your words fill me. Help me to turn my life around, away from being self-centered to serving God and neighbor. May my transformation in Christ draw others to you and to your way of life in this world.

Listening to God's Words
With an Open Heart

The risen Lord speaks: My brother or sister, hear what I say, for my words bring true life and my wisdom goes way beyond anything you can learn anyplace else. Indeed, my words "are spirit and life" (John 6:63) and cannot be measured by human standards. Listen to my words in the silence of your heart and receive them with an open mind and with love. Don't think you can use my words for self-centered purposes, however, or to make other people admire you.

The follower of Christ speaks: How happy and blessed is the one whom you instruct, O Lord, and the one to whom you give help in difficult times. For the one you teach and guide will no longer feel that life has no meaning or purpose.

The risen Lord speaks: Even from the beginning of the world, I have taught those who listen to me, and even now I continue to speak to those who will listen. Sad to say, however, that many do not listen to me but listen to their own empty thoughts instead.

Most people don't want to trouble themselves to distinguish between what's good, true, and beautiful in the world and what's empty or even self-destructive. It takes a mature, clear-thinking person to do that. Many are more ready to listen to nonsense than to my word. Much—though certainly not all—of what the dominant popular culture promises has no real value, yet a great many people swallow the popular culture hook, line, and sinker. All that I promise is good, true, beautiful, and eternal, yet most people's hearts remain indifferent to what I offer. How many people do you know who serve and obey me with the enthusiasm with which they respond to the empty promises of mass media advertising? For empty nonsense people will make great sacrifices and work many hours each week, but for eternal things many will hardly lift a finger.

Allow my words to dwell in your heart of hearts and think about what I say, for you will need my words when hard times come. If you find any of my words difficult to comprehend, you will understand when I make my presence felt, and I do this in a couple of ways. First, you can feel my presence when hard times come and you feel anxious or fearful. Second, you can feel my presence when you calm yourself and enter into a prayerful attitude, for then I can comfort and console you. Every day I offer you two lessons. First, I remind you of your weakness and need for me. Second, I give you encouragement and remind you to never stop trusting in my care for you.

Prayer for the Grace To Be a Faithful Follower of Christ

God, my loving father, from you I came and to you I return. In many ways I am an unfaithful servant. I remember, loving God, that apart from you I have nothing and can do nothing. You are the source of all that is good, just, beautiful, and holy. From you all things come, and all things are present in you. Only those who refuse your love do you send away with nothing. Help me to welcome your love into my life.

How can I resist the inclination to be fearful and anxious and not trust in you unless you encourage and support me every day? Loving God, teach me how to do your will in all things. Help me to welcome your love into my heart every day, for you are my all in all. You know me as I truly am, and you have known me since before the world came into existence and before I was born. Help me to be your faithful follower and friend in all things and at all times. Amen.

CHAPTER 4

Living With God in Spirit and in Truth

The risen Lord speaks: My loved one, always walk with me in truth, and always seek me with a sincere heart. Whoever walks with me in spirit and truth will be protected from evil, and the truth will liberate him or her from those who lie and mislead people with empty promises. The truth sets you free, so you are already free and you don't need to be concerned about empty, misleading messages from mass media advertising.

The follower of Christ speaks: Lord, what you say is certainly the truth, and so I ask you to let it be with me as you have said. Let your truth be my only guide, and let your truth guard and preserve me all the days of my life until I pass through the veil from this life to the next. Let your truth liberate me from love for the wrong things so that I may live my life in you with a heart free from all darkness.

The risen Lord speaks: I am the Truth, and I will teach and guide you in all things to what is good, true, and beautiful. Remember that you often act out of fear and selfishness instead of acting from trust and loving charity. Remember that only with me can you expect to have a life worth living and a life filled with meaning and purpose. And even then, don't forget that all you have that is good, true, and beautiful is from me.

Let my truth alone please you, and rededicate yourself each morning to the love of God and neighbor, which is the purpose of your existence. Fear nothing more than becoming forgetful of this, even more than losing all your possessions and your life itself. For a life apart from the love of God and neighbor is an empty, sad life.

Some people go through the motions of living as a disciple of mine, but they are not sincere. Their so-called faith makes no real difference in how they live their lives. For them, "believing in God" is a mere opinion that makes no real difference in their lives at all.

Others, because their faith in me is real, are enlightened and care only for the love of God and loving charity toward their neighbors. No matter what their work may be, and no matter how they make their living, their ultimate concern is the love of God and neighbor, and they nourish their lives by participating in the life of my people, the Church. They are prayerful people, and they strive to trust completely in my love. Knowing that their ultimate destiny is joy, they give little attention to the fear and anxiety that they sometimes feel.

CHAPTER 5

The Wonderful Effects
of God's Love

The follower of Christ speaks: God, our loving father and father of our Lord Jesus Christ, I thank and praise you, for you have chosen to think of me, helpless as I am. God of all mercy and encouragement, I thank you for sometimes giving me the renewed spirit that I need to carry on in your presence. I give you endless thanks, loving Father, along with your only son, the risen Lord, who nourishes me with his whole self in the Eucharist, and with your Holy Spirit, who comforts and guides me.

Loving God, when I become aware of your presence in my deepest center, when I become aware that you are always with me and within me, I feel great joy and gratitude to you. You are all that matters to me and the greatest joy of my heart. You are my greatest hope and the one to whom I can turn no matter how bad things look.

Because I sometimes have difficulty trying to trust in your love and care for me and for those I love, I need your support and encouragement all the more. I know you are always with me, but help me to be aware of this more often and teach me to live consciously in your presence more of the time. Teach me your ways. Liberate me from the tendency to act out of fear instead of trust.

Love is the ultimate reality, for you are love. Love makes difficulties and hardships easier to cope with. The love of Christ matters more than anything else and inspires us to live in ways that attract others to him and to his people, the Church. Love wants to do good things for you, our God. Love wants to be free and not let itself be dragged down by fears and anxieties.

Nothing is more delightful than love, nothing has more strength, nothing is more wonderful or more resilient, and nothing is better than love on this earth or in eternity, for love comes from God and leads us to God.

The person in love flies higher than a kite, runs without effort, and is filled with joy. Being in love is freeing so that nothing can hold you back, so you're more than willing to give your all for the sake of the beloved. To be in love is to be united to the one from whom all good things come. Therefore, love can do all things and is successful where those without love grow weak and give up.

To be in love with God is to love other people, and to be in love with another person is to be in love with God. Make my love deeper, my God, so that I may learn to love in spirit and in truth and not just when love feels good. Let love possess me and let me rise above selfishness to love in all circumstances.

Let me love you more than myself, O God, and let me have a proper love of my neighbor and myself for your sake. For love acts quickly, is honest, prayerful, ready to please others, and joyful. Love is strong, patient, wise in practical matters, reliable, ready to sacrifice for God and neighbor, and never selfish, for selfishness is the opposite of love.

Love never takes foolish risks, seeks only the truth, and stands up for justice. Love is never weak, erratic, self-indulgent, or interested in triviality. Love is morally pure, decent, and modest. Love is steady, calm, and has no interest in sensuality for its own sake.

Love is submissive to the loved one without wanting the other to dominate. At the same time, being in love does not preclude sorrows and trials! Love bears burdens patiently and with strength. If you're not ready to accept conflict and hard times while being faithful to the loved one, you are no true lover at all. True love, for the sake of the beloved—whether God or another person—is ready and willing to accept hard times faithful in love, and it doesn't matter how hard life may be. Love persists.

CHAPTER 6

How to Tell
When Love Is True

The risen Lord speaks: My brother or sister, so far you are still a work in progress.

The follower of Christ speaks: What do you mean, Lord Jesus?

The risen Lord speaks: You are a work in progress because— and you have to admit that this is true—whenever you run up against even a little opposition or some difficulty, you feel sorry for yourself and try to find some way to get out of whatever is facing you. A true and courageous lover hangs in there and does what needs to be done. Remember this: just as I am the true lover's delight in the good times, I am also the lover's delight in times of difficulty, stress and anxiety.

A savvy lover thinks not so much about what he or she gets from the other as about the love that inspires the giving. The lover is more aware of the other's love than the value of the gift the other gives, and the true lover values the beloved far above any gifts the lover may receive from the other. A true lover is never satisfied with the gift received but desires above all union with God, the ultimate giver, and peaceable relationships with others.

Sometimes you may feel out of touch with me and with my saints. Don't let that discourage you; just keep on keeping on. For my life, or grace, working in you is but a small taste of what you will enjoy fully when you pass from this world to your heavenly home. Don't rely much on feelings of any kind, for they shift easily from pleasant to unpleasant and back again. Just keep on doing what you know is right and good.

To ignore thoughts and ideas that you know are wrong indicates that you have made some progress in the life of faith. So don't let odd-ball ideas that come into your head worry you at all. Just let them pass and go about your business. Remember to turn to God our father and to me often during your day, with simple words of prayer from your heart.

You need to realize that your tendency to do good is often obstructed by your tendency to laziness and indifference. Ask your favorite saint to pray for you that you might have strength. This is a wonderfully Christian spiritual practice no one should overlook. Try to be quiet and reserved in your manner.

When you sometimes fail to act like a person of true Christian faith, hope, and loving charity, humbly ask for God's merciful forgiveness, and—if appropriate—for your neighbor's forgiveness, too. Then move on with your life. And, when you next have the opportunity, don't forget to take advantage of the blessings that come from the sacrament of reconciliation.

CHAPTER 7

Divine Life in You and the Virtue of Humility

The risen Lord speaks: My friend and companion, if you sometimes feel very close to me, don't let it go to your head. You're no great saint yet, you know. And certainly, do not go around talking about how close you feel to me. People will think you have a screw loose. Just let feelings of closeness to me be a reminder to trust in me in all things. For spiritual adulthood doesn't mean having such feelings. Rather, it means being able to go on living your faith, and being dedicated to the love of God and neighbor regardless of how you feel. Love is primarily an act of the will, not pleasant feelings. If you can go on being a prayerful person, and go on loving God and neighbor even when you don't feel like it, then you are becoming spiritually grown up. Many people become discouraged and get spiritually lazy when things don't go as they would like.

Those who are inexperienced in the life of faith can easily mess up their lives if they refuse to listen to the wise advice of more experienced people. If such people refuse to listen to good advice and follow their own inclinations instead, they are sure to come to an unpleasant end. People who think they already know it all don't have enough humility to let others offer guidance. It's better to be ignorant and be humble about it than to know everything and have no humility.

The one who wants to have security above all else, regardless of circumstances, is likely to be the most unhappy when the going gets difficult. If you know how to trust unconditionally in God, you will be at peace whether your life is easy or difficult.

Here is what you need to remember: when everything is light and peace, remember how you will feel when you no longer have light and peace. Then, when this happens, remember that light and peace will return. All that is important is for you to go on being faithful to me and to love of God and neighbor, no matter how you feel.

The difficult times are often more helpful to attaining an adult faith than if you always have things go your way. Your true character isn't determined by being popular, or by attaining great honors, or by accumulating much knowledge. Rather, what matters is whether you are truly dedicated to your faith and to the love of God and neighbor. That's what it's all about.

CHAPTER 8

On Having an Accurate Opinion of Yourself

The follower of Christ speaks: If I have an inflated opinion of myself, you, Lord, are not impressed. If I have a proper self-love, however, that is based on a deep realization of your love for me, then I will have a healthy sense of self-esteem. It is only in my deepest center that you reveal to me the truth about myself and the truth of your presence in and all around me at all times. You are always ready to lift me up and encourage me when I feel down and out.

It is your love, Lord Jesus, that makes it possible for me to live a good and worthwhile life. You help me to have a true love for God and neighbor, and you care for me when I am in danger.

By indulging in a selfish form of self-love, which I should not have done, I actually lost my deepest self. But by seeking you in all things, and loving you with my whole being, I found both you and my deepest self. And, through this love, I have become more conscious of your presence in the world.

God, may you be blessed in all times and places. Through baptism into Christ, I am your adopted child. Therefore, you look upon me with great love, and you never stop doing good toward even those who turn away from you. Help us all to turn back to you so that we may return to our dedication to love you and our neighbor in all things.

CHAPTER 9

Remembering That God Is Our Beginning and Our End

The risen Lord speaks: My child, if you want to have a life that is truly blessed, then I must be your ultimate concern and final goal in all things. When you think of everything in terms of your relationship with me, you purify your motives and actions, which all too often are motivated by selfishness. When you act selfishly, even in small matters, your true self begins to fade and grow weak.

Therefore, think of all things in terms of your faith relationship with me, for everything you have comes from me. Understand that all things need to be understood in terms of me as their beginning and end, for all things were created through me.

All people, whether great or insignificant in the eyes of the world, whether rich, middle class, or poor, get their life and breath from me, and those who serve me freely receive "grace upon grace" (John 1:16). But those who seek to gain peace and security from anything but me or who seek delight from anything other than my presence in things will never have true joy. Rather, they will encounter one obstacle after another and end up tangled in all kinds of trouble and grief.

Don't let that happen to you. Think of everything in your life in relation to your faith relationship with me. For I have given you everything that you have, including all your talents and gifts and even your handicaps and weaknesses, which are gifts, too, if you only see them in the context of your faith relationship with me. The only appropriate attitude to have toward me is one of gratitude for all that I have given you.

This is the overarching truth that puts everything in its proper context: if you welcome my divine life and love into your heart, you will have no reason to envy anyone else or complain about your own situation or act out of selfishness. My love overcomes all self-ishness and obstacles and deepens your capacity to love God and neighbor and even your enemy.

If you are level-headed, you will find joy and peace in me alone, and you will trust in me alone.

CHAPTER 10

The Joy of Serving God

The follower of Christ speaks: I will speak to you again, Lord, and will not be silent. I will say in the hearing of my God, who is closer to me than I am to myself, that your love is beyond imagining, and you will never cease loving those who put their trust in you.

You revealed your limitless love for me by bringing me into existence from nothing. When I gave you little more than empty words, you drew me back to you so that I might serve you, and you taught me how to love you and my companions in this world.

O my Lord and source of eternal love, how can I forget you when you continued to remember me even when I forgot you and indulged in all kinds of addictions, escapism, and selfishness? How can I ever repay you for your grace in my life? You give everyone the grace to follow you in the particular calling they receive from you, whether in marriage, single life, vowed religious life, or the ordained priesthood. You gave me the grace to follow you in my ordinary everyday life, and for this I thank you endlessly. Give this same grace to all, Lord!

Everything that I have belongs to you, Lord Jesus, and with all that I have I serve you. But the truth is that you serve me rather than me serving you. How amazing this is! For in all that I am and all that I do, you hold me in existence and keep me close to yourself.

What can I give you in return for the countless gifts you give me in every moment? If only I could serve you adequately in return, even for one day! All I can do is to thank you, continue to try to do my best, and ask for your mercy and forgiveness for all the ways I fail to measure up to your love for me.

All the same, I see it as a great honor to be called your follower, and I thank you for the grace of following you in your Church, holy and imperfect as it is. I thank you for the support of the Eucharist and the other sacraments of your Church that nourish me on my way. I thank you for the holy Scriptures in which your Word guides and feeds my heart and mind.

It is a great honor to be able to see all of creation present in your holy presence and to see all things in relation to you. Those who freely give themselves to your service know your eternal and sacred life in their deepest selves. Those who relate all things to you, including the pleasures of the body, because of their love for you enjoy the comfort and support of the Holy Spirit. Those who freely choose to walk in this world only in your presence and participate in the affairs of this world in your name only have the greatest freedom of heart and soul.

How happy are those who serve God in all that they do, for in this they become truly free and grow spiritually strong and healthy. How wonderful it is to serve God in whatever way of life a person follows, for it makes a person equal to the angels, a joy to God, and a role model for other people. This way of service is desirable above all things, for it gains for us the greatest good of all: a loving intimacy with God that results in a joy that will last even beyond life in this world.

CHAPTER 11

Learning To Be Aware of and in Charge of Your Deepest Desires

The risen Lord speaks: My beloved child, you still have a lot to learn about being my follower and servant.

The follower of Christ speaks: What are you talking about, Lord Jesus?

The risen Lord speaks: You need to seek my will in all things and stop being so self-centered. You often express a desire to act on my behalf and do my will in all things, but your motive is still basically your own self-interest. Yes, you need to have a proper self-love, but even when it comes to taking care of yourself—which you must do if you are to have the resources you need to care for others—your motive must be unselfish. Once your motive is to serve God and neighbor in all things, then you will make progress in the spiritual life.

Therefore, take care to rely more on me than on your own devices. Always turn to me in prayer before you run off in all directions with your grand and glorious plans. Otherwise, you may later find that you are unhappy with the results of your efforts.

Not everything that seems like a good idea should be acted upon, nor should you avoid acting on every idea that is different from what you feel that you want. Even when it comes to doing good, sometimes you need to restrain yourself; otherwise, being too eager may lead to exhausting yourself, and then what good are you to others? At the same time, your lack of control over yourself may offend others, and then their objections may discourage you and make you feel like giving up. Sometimes it's necessary to resist your tendency to want to dash about "doing good" all over the place and listen, instead, to common sense.

Learning To Be Patient and Overcoming Inappropriate Tendencies

The follower of Christ speaks: God, so often I encounter obstacles and opposition, and I see that I need to learn to be more patient both with myself and with others. No matter what I do to try to be more at peace, I find that I still end up experiencing conflict and regret.

The risen Lord speaks: That's the way it goes. I don't want you to waste your energy looking for perfect peace or trying to avoid conflict at all costs. At the same time, I want you to have peace even in the midst of difficulties and hard times.

Material riches come and go without bringing any real satisfaction to those who possess them. Real happiness comes only from abandoning yourself to my love. If you really want to have the peace that only I can give, know that this peace comes not instead of troubles and difficulties but in the midst of troubles and difficulties. The more you find me in all things, in your pleasures and joys as well as your troubles and anxieties, the closer you will be to me.

CHAPTER 13

Quiet Obedience According to the Example of the Lord Jesus

The risen Lord speaks: My child, one of life's most difficult lessons is learning to be obedient to my will, which is your only peace. And how can you know my will? It comes to you in the ordinary events of your everyday life. First, in the requirements and joys of your calling—whether to marriage, single life, religious life, or the priesthood—my grace makes it possible for you to see what needs to be done, and that is my will for you. Then, in the requirements and joys of your daily work, do your work as an expression of love for God and neighbor. This is my will. If you cannot love God and neighbor through your daily work, seek the wise counsel of some spiritual and practical-minded person to help you find my will for you.

Sometimes it's because you are still so self-centered that you find it difficult to give yourself to my will as it comes to you in your everyday life. No daily work, and no life, is free from stress and frustration. Learn to recognize that it is my will that you try to be faithful to your calling, even in the midst of stress and conflict. Love is only real when it remains faithful through the hard times, too. Grow up! Sometimes the only good advice when you indulge in self-pity is to get over it.

Always remember that you are precious to me. I have loved you since before the beginning of the universe, and my love for you will never end.

CHAPTER 14

You Never Know
What Life Will Bring

The follower of Christ speaks: God, I am amazed and delighted by the greatness of your loving goodness to me, to all people, and to all of creation. Thank you for the great blessing of being alive and being able to enjoy being a part of all that you have made.

No one can be spiritually strong and healthy, O Lord, if you do not fill them with your divine life. No human wisdom is of any use to us unless it comes from you. No strength is enough unless you supply it. No sexual integrity is safe unless you protect it. No commitment to act with justice and truth will succeed unless you help us to keep that commitment. Only because you are always with us, closer to us than we are to ourselves, can we hope to find meaning in this world and eternal life in the next.

Should a beautiful work of music or art get the credit for its own beauty? Of course not! Rather, the composer or artist should get the credit. Can the one whose heart is transparent to your holiness, O God, brag about it? Nothing can make such a person, whom truth has united to himself, brag about it. Neither will the person who has placed his or her hope in God be distracted by the praise of other people. For those who speak such praises are only human themselves, on pilgrimage in this world. Only God's truth will last forever.

CHAPTER 15

How to Pray for
What You Want

The risen Lord speaks: My child, always remember to pray like this: "Lord, if what I ask for is pleasing to you and good for me in your eyes, then let it be. If it will attract others to you, O Lord, then let this be done in your name. But if you see that it will be harmful to me and be of no help in attracting others to you, then take this desire away from me."

The truth is, just because something looks good and praiseworthy to you, that doesn't mean that it comes from the Holy Spirit. I see the big picture, while you can see only part of it. I see past, present, and future, while you see only part of the present. No matter how good what you pray for seems to be, leave it in my hands and trust in my wisdom and grace.

Whenever it enters your heart to pray for something that seems very good, ask for it with humility, but trust in me to do what's best for all concerned. Give up your own will and pray that only my will may be done, no matter how much anguish it gives you to think of not getting what you ask for. Pray thus: "Lord, you know what is best for me. Let all things be done according to your will. Lead me wherever you will. I want to be your servant in all things. I want to live not for myself, but for you!"

Look for Lasting Peace
and Consolation in God Alone

The follower of Christ speaks: The perfect peace and contentment I seek will never be mine in this life, but only in the life to come. Even if I had all the comfort and security the world has to offer, and even if I were the richest person in the world, the peace of mind and heart that comes from such things would not last very long at all. For in my deepest center, there is a hunger and thirst that only you, my God, can satisfy, and only in eternity will this hunger and thirst be satisfied completely.

If you ignore this wisdom, and crave the good things of this world more than you should, you will certainly be disappointed. Make proper use of the good things to be found in this life, but desire even now, and even more, the blessings and grace of eternity. The things of this world will never completely satisfy you because you were not created to enjoy them alone. All the comforts and pleasures of this world ultimately fail to satisfy, but true and blessed is the consolation and joy received in your heart from God alone.

The person of true faith carries the risen Lord Jesus in his or her heart at all times and in all places, and prays to him: "Lord Jesus, my risen Savior, stay with me always, no matter where I am. Help me to find you in all the good things of this world and in all the people I encounter each day, loved ones and strangers alike. Amen."

We Should Leave All
Our Worries With God

The risen Lord speaks: My child, trust that I know what is best for you. Let me lead you where I will. Your vision is limited, and your thinking is limited, and you tend to evaluate things from a narrow perspective.

The follower of Christ speaks: I know that what you say is true, Lord Jesus, and you care for me far more than I can ever care for myself, and anyone who will not give his or her concerns to you will be very insecure, indeed.

Lord, as long as I remain firmly committed to you, do what you want with me. For whatever you do with me can only be good for myself and for all concerned. If you think it's best for me to be in darkness and not know what the future will bring, let that be the way things are for me. If you want me to be in the light, again I want only what you want. If you choose to comfort me with spiritual or material comforts, may you be praised. And if trials come my way, may you still be praised. Help me to use such difficulties to purify my faith and grow closer to you.

The risen Lord speaks: My child, this is the best attitude for you to have if you wish to live in union with me in this world. You must be just as ready to put up with hardships as you are to experience security and joy; just as ready to be poor and insecure as wealthy and in possession of financial and material forms of security.

The follower of Christ speaks: Lord Jesus, I will gladly accept for your sake whatever comes my way. I am just as ready to live with good or bad times, sweet or bitter experiences, joy or sorrow, and I ask you to draw me closer to you by means of whatever comes my way.

Keep me safe from anything and everything that damages my relationships with you and those with whom I live and work most closely. Then I will fear nothing, not even death or oblivion, because no matter what happens to me, nothing can hurt me as long as I cling to your love.

CHAPTER 18

We Must Patiently Tolerate Hardship Just as Jesus Did Before Us

The risen Lord speaks: My child, I came into this world to liberate and heal you. I did this out of love, not because there was any need to do so. I wanted you to learn patience and to grow into a full human being, just as I did. During my lifetime, I knew the human love of Mary and Joseph, which was a great blessing. I also had friends, though sometimes they failed to grasp the meaning of true friendship. But also, from the moment of my birth right up to the moment of my death on the cross, I had more suffering and anxiety than you will ever have. During my life on this earth, I was poor. Especially in the last few years of my life, people often opposed me and lied about me. Out of compassion I tolerated insults and humiliation. When I was kind, I received ingratitude; when I performed miracles, I was held in contempt; and when I spoke the truth, I was criticized.

The follower of Christ speaks: Lord Jesus, you lived your earthly life with patience and with kindness and tolerance for all, even those who were despised by the "respectable" people of your time. In this, above all, you obeyed your father's will. So it is only right that I should patiently obey your will in all things and not complain when things don't go as I want them to go. Sometimes we find life to be burdensome, but this is the phase of our eternal existence during which we are supposed to learn to love God and neighbor and overcome, by God's grace, our selfishness and lack of trust. Your life, death, and resurrection, Lord, have made this life lighter than it would be otherwise, and the inspiring example of your many saints adds to our hope.

What gratitude I owe you, Lord, for so kindly leading me, and all who follow you, on the straight and good path to your eternal home. What would we do if we did not have your light to follow as we live our lives?

CHAPTER 19

Tolerating Injuries Is the Proof of Real Patience

The risen Lord speaks: Whether your hardships are big or small, try to bear them all patiently. If you are determined to put up with such things patiently, you will be acting as I did. Besides, you will find your difficulties and sufferings easier to bear if you work at having the right attitude toward them.

Bear patiently with the hardships inflicted on you by others. Don't say, "I can't possibly put up with this kind of treatment from a person such as that. It's not fair." Instead, go to the person with whom you have a hard time getting along and tell him or her about your experience and your feelings without accusations. Then see if you can't get along better in the future.

The follower of Christ speaks: Lord Jesus, help me to do with your grace what is impossible for me to do if left to my own resources. You know how little I can do on my own when some small hardship comes my way and how I go all to pieces when that happens. Help me to grow up spiritually and not be one of the great whiners of the world.

CHAPTER 20

Admitting Our Weakness in Facing the Hardships of This Life

The follower of Christ speaks: Lord Jesus, I readily admit my weaknesses to you, and I admit my frequent choices that harm my relationships with you and those with whom I live and work most closely. So often it is such a small difficulty or temptation that gets me down. I make up my mind to act courageously, and when a little obstacle comes along, I get anxious or upset all out of proportion. I often fail to do what is right.

Great and good God of Israel and our loving father have pity on the fears, anxieties, and sorrows of your humble servant and help me in all that I do. Strengthen me with your grace so that my deepest and most real self may come more and more to life and so that my weak and superficial self does not have the most control.

What a life! Help me to understand that troubles and anxieties are but reminders that I must always trust in you and that our ultimate destiny is beyond this world of time and space in the great mystery of eternal love.

CHAPTER 21

Our Ultimate Security Is in God

The follower of Christ speaks: My soul, my deepest self, you must always find your security only in the Lord Jesus, for in him is the only ultimately reliable security to be had in both this world and the next.

Lord Jesus, help me to place my trust in your loving concern for me rather than in any possessions or financial security that this world has to offer. Help me to be realistic and responsible and to do my work the best I can. More importantly, help me to realize that in the end you are the only one in whom I can place my trust—beyond health and good looks and all the honor and praise this world may confer upon me; beyond power and influence, education and ability; beyond happiness and joy; beyond wealth and fame; beyond all affluence; beyond hopes and promises, rewards and desires; beyond all the gifts that are in your power to give; beyond all the gladness and joy that are in our power to feel; beyond saints and angels; beyond all things visible and invisible; beyond anything which is not you, O God.

Lord Jesus, risen Christ, ruler of all creation, who will give me the wings of genuine liberty except you? You are the only true comfort for the pilgrim soul, and I am speechless before you. Yet I will let my silence speak to you from the depths of my heart. I long for the light of your presence to give me refreshment. Help me to see your face which is always before me, and set me free.

The risen Lord speaks: I am here, and I am always with you, closer than you are to yourself because you are open to my presence. Never forget that I will never abandon you, even when you find it impossible to feel that I am with you.

CHAPTER 22

On Thinking About God's Many Gifts to Us

The follower of Christ speaks: Lord Jesus, instruct my heart to understand your ways and show me how to be united to you in all that I do. Help me to know what is your will for me and help me to recognize and be thankful for all your gifts to me.

All of our talents and abilities, and even our weaknesses and handicaps of body, mind, and spirit, come as blessings from you and reveal your goodness, generosity, and love if we are open to your presence in them. All that we have can help us to serve you in this life. One person may receive more gifts, another less; but all gifts are from you, and apart from you no one can possess anything at all.

If a person receives more gifts or talents than others, he or she has no right to brag or act superior or take those gifts or talents for granted. No one has a right to look down upon others or hold them in contempt for any reason whatsoever. Rather, this person should, in the silence of his or her heart, give all the credit to God, who is the source of all good.

If you receive fewer gifts or not extraordinary gifts, that makes no difference to God. Do not envy the one who has special gifts or talents. Rather, give thanks to God for the gifts or talents that person has received and pray that he or she will use them wisely and well.

CHAPTER 23

How To Have Peace of Mind and Heart

The risen Lord speaks: Whatever you do, and as long as you have a choice, always choose to have less rather than more. The dominant popular culture is not without good, but at the same time it constantly tries to convince you that you never have enough of anything. Don't believe such foolishness. Never think of yourself as better than anyone else. Always pray that the will of God may be done in your life. You will find that the one who does all this lives a life of peace and contentment.

The follower of Christ speaks: Lord Jesus, your words are few, but what you say is perfect. If only I could do what you say, I would not be so easily upset or depressed. Whenever I feel bummed out and have no peace, I find that I have forgotten this wisdom that you speak.

You can do all things, and you always love me no matter how I am feeling. Increase the gift of your divine life in me, risen Christ, so that I can act on what you teach and thus receive the fullness of healing and liberation in this world and the next.

A Prayer Against Self-Defeating Thoughts

God, help me to know with all my heart and soul that at all times I am permeated by your love for me. Fears and anxieties so often fill my mind. How can I survive?

"I will support and guide you on your way," says the Lord, "so that the fears and anxieties that trouble you will vanish and bother you no more."

O Lord Jesus, do as you say, and may all my fears and anxieties leave me and be replaced by complete trust in your loving care for me. My only hope and comfort is to remember how close you are to me, even in all my troubles and difficulties, to trust you, to turn to you from my heart, and to wait until I feel your love once more.

A Prayer for True Enlightenment

Good Lord Jesus, give me enlightenment of mind and heart by filling me with the brightness of your grace. Drive out all darkness from my heart. Help me to resist putting myself down and not to give in to self-defeating thoughts. Help me to remember and rejoice in your great love for me no matter what may happen. When I am upset or depressed, say to my heart, "Be still."

Raise up this soul of mine that is so often weighed down with worries and sorrows. Let the light of heaven fill my heart and mind so that my thinking may be clear and always trusting in you. Help me to see things as you see them, as in the light of day and not as in the darkness of night. Fill me with devotion to you and with a desire to turn to you often in prayer. Help me to remember at all times that you have united yourself to me with an unbreakable bond of love and that you alone can satisfy my yearning for love and fulfillment.

CHAPTER 24

On Not Being Preoccupied
With Useless Cares and Concerns

The risen Lord speaks: My child, don't burden yourself with useless cares and concerns. All you need to be concerned about is whether you are following me. Don't occupy yourself with what others do or say. You need have no interest in other people's affairs. Just leave it all to me and go about your own business—which is the love of God and neighbor. Maintain your own peace of mind and don't attempt to stick your nose into other people's business.

Have no interest in trying to gain the illusion of fame or in trying to win the approval and attention of others. To do so is to fill your heart with darkness. I will gladly speak to your inmost heart and give you my own life in abundance, if only you will open the door of your heart. Live quietly and carefully and turn to me often in prayer.

CHAPTER 25

The Basis of Unshakable Peace
and Spiritual Maturity

The risen Lord speaks: My child, remember that I have said: "Peace I leave with you; my peace I give to you. I do not give to you as the world gives" (John 14:27).

Everyone wants peace, but not everyone wants to do what is required in order to have true peace. Those who are humble and gentle have my peace in their hearts, and you will have my peace if you are very patient. If you participate in the Eucharist often and listen to my word and act on it, you will enjoy great peace of mind and heart.

At all times and in all places, be aware of what you are doing and saying and have no concern for anything except to please me rather than to gain the approval of other people. As far as the words and actions of others are concerned, restrain yourself from making impulsive judgments and keep your nose out of other people's business. This will help to calm your inner disturbances. Of course, you can't expect to be free from all trials and troubles during your earthly life. No one is free from all distress and conflict for long. Perfect peace comes only in eternity.

Therefore, don't make the mistake of thinking that you have found true peace just because you aren't aware, at the moment, of any difficulties or conflicts. Never imagine that God loves you more than others. Feelings of spiritual devotion and calm don't mean that you have become some near-perfect spiritual being. While pleasant, such feelings are temporary and are not the basis of spiritual maturity. One does not prove his or her virtue during easy times.

You will know that you have attained some degree of spiritual adulthood when you can surrender your whole self to the love of God and neighbor, whether things are going well for you or not. Go on thanking God cheerfully in good times or in hard times. The more you can disregard yourself, the more you will have abundant peace.

CHAPTER 26

The Superiority of a Free Mind That Comes From Being a Prayerful Person

The follower of Christ speaks: Lord Jesus, spiritual maturity makes it possible to keep one's mind focused on the love of God and neighbor and to live from one day to the next without being fearful or anxious about anything. This is not because one is insensitive, but because one is not controlled by a craving or desire for things that fail to satisfy the heart.

Merciful God, I pray that you may keep me from being overwhelmed by the cares and worries of this life. Keep me from seeking pleasure for its own sake and save me from defeat and despair when I am worried or anxious.

I don't ask you to rescue me from the superficial things that the foolish want so much, but from the normal fears and anxieties of life that so easily drag me down and keep me from enjoying the freedom and healing I would so much like to experience more often.

O God, help me to recognize your presence in and through all things. Save me from being defeated in this world; don't let me be led astray. Help me to have clarity of vision so that I may see you in everything you have made, including myself, all those with whom I live and work, and those I encounter only briefly each day.

Grant that I may give you thanks for all your blessings that most of the time I take for granted: for food and drink, for whatever health I enjoy, for clothing and shelter. Help me to remember that all these things are also reminders that your care for me will carry me and protect me, even in passing through the veil from this world to eternity. Help me to not seek more than I need and to use all things in moderation. I pray that throughout my life in this world you will guide and teach me. Keep me from anything that harms my relationships with you, with other people, and with the earth.

CHAPTER 27

Being Self-Centered Keeps Us From the Greatest Good

The risen Lord speaks: My child, in order to receive everything you must give everything. You must give up ownership even of your very self. Understand that being self-centered does you more harm than anything the world can do to you. There is a proper kind of self-love, one that is not self-centered, that you must cultivate. You must nourish and care for yourself, but you must do this in order to be able to care for and nourish others. For you can't give what you don't have. This is the meaning of the commandment of the Lord to love God with your whole self and your neighbor as yourself.

Do not crave things that are not good for you and do not retain possession of anything that is an obstacle to your inner freedom. If you are in the grip of a self-destructive addiction, have the humility and self-respect to get help to liberate yourself from that addiction.

You will never be happy or at peace as long as your happiness depends on anything outside of yourself, such as possessions, a high level of affluence, or financial security. Even if you attain what you desire, there will always be something to disappoint you.

You will find little advantage from living in a certain place if the spirit of prayerfulness and other-centeredness is missing, and a peace that depends on possessions or wealth will not last long. If you do not rest in me, you can have all the money and possessions in the world and you will still not be happy. Yes, you need a certain degree of financial security, but know that the more generous you are with others, the more generous the good God will be with you.

A Prayer for Simplicity of Heart and Divine Wisdom

O God, make me strong with the grace of the Holy Spirit. Strengthen me with a strength that reaches my deepest self so that I may rid my heart of all useless cares and anxieties. Help me not to crave things that do not last and teach me to know that all things pass away and that I am passing with them. For nothing that the sun shines upon is lasting, but everything here reflects your divine goodness. How wise is the person who knows this!

Lord Jesus Christ, grant me the wisdom of the gospel so that I may learn to be aware of your presence in the world. Teach me to delight in you and love you above all things and to value all other things according to the place they have in your divine plan.

Give me the common sense to disregard flattery and the patience and skill to tolerate and work through conflict. It is true wisdom to remain at peace amid other people's words that are so unreliable. Thus we shall be able to go through this life in safety and stay on the straight and narrow path.

CHAPTER 28

On Disregarding Those Who Speak Against You

The risen Lord speaks: My child, you must not get upset if some people have a poor opinion of you and say things that are not true. Just remember that the only opinion of you that matters is my opinion of you.

If you are walking the path of the inner life, you will not give much thought to words that come and go like the breeze. It takes wisdom to remain quiet when times are troubling, to turn to me in your heart—which is where I always live, and not to let the opinions of other people upset you.

You must not let peace of mind and heart depend upon what others say. Whether they judge you in pleasant or unpleasant ways, that doesn't make you any different from what you really are.

True peace can only be found in me, and the secret of deep and lasting peace of mind and heart is to be indifferent to whether you please other people. Do not fear displeasing others as long as you are doing what you know is right. It is your affection for things unworthy of your heart and your foolish anxieties that deprive you of peace in your heart.

CHAPTER 29

In the Middle of Worries and Anxieties, We Must Rely Entirely Upon God

The follower of Christ speaks: May your name, O Lord, be honored forever, for times of trouble and anxiety come to us all and cannot be avoided. Such times are inescapable, and so I must turn to you as my only reliable source of help and security. You can help hard times become, in fact, a blessing for me.

O Lord, difficulties are upon me now, and I have no peace in my heart. I find it hard to put up with all my troubles. Loving Father, what can I say? Deliver me and rescue me, O Lord, when I have been brought low. Grant me patience, and help me, O my God, and I will not be afraid regardless of how heavy the burden I must carry.

Now, in the middle of all my troubles, I say, "O Lord, may your will be done, for only in your will is my peace."

CHAPTER 30

On Asking for God's Help and Believing That His Grace Is Always With You

The risen Lord speaks: My child, I am the Lord, and there is no strength like mine in times of trouble and distress. I am always with you, so turn to me when things are hard for you.

The greatest obstacle to receiving the comfort of heaven is how slow you are to turn to me in prayer. Before you even begin turning to me, first you look for help and comfort in all kinds of other places and try to find peace and security in things your senses can perceive. Then—surprise, surprise—you find little help in any of these things. Finally, when you have tried everything else you can think of, you turn to me. You must realize that I am the only one who can save you if only you put your trust in me. Apart from me there is no lasting help, no advice you can count on, and no healing that will last.

When your deepest self revives after your troubles pass, you will grow strong and peaceful again under the clear sky of my mercies. I am always closer to you than you are to yourself. I restore all things not just to their former state but make them even better than they were before. Nothing is too difficult for me. Stand firmly and don't give up hope. Be patient and courageous, for assistance will come to you in due time. Wait for me, and I will be there to heal you.

This panic you feel is nothing but a temptation, and the fears that you are so anxious about have no basis in reality. What is the good of worrying that terrible things might happen? That only piles one misery on top of another. There is no point in being fearful about the future when the things you are afraid that might happen may well never happen at all. It is a human weakness to be misled by this kind of thinking. For heaven's sake, don't ever think that you have been abandoned by me, even if you find yourself in the middle of troubles and distress. This is just the way life is.

If you were wise, and could see things as they really are, you would never become sad when you experience troubles or anxieties. Rely on me and trust in my loving care, and everything will come out right. Think back on the countless times you were afraid that awful things were going to happen—and then they didn't happen at all. This is just another one of those times. Or think about times when bad things happened to you and then they turned out to carry blessings you never could have imagined.

CHAPTER 31

On Finding Reminders and Reflections of God in All Things

The follower of Christ speaks: O Lord, I need far more of your divine life, your grace, in me than I have now if I am ever to be able to trust in you as completely as you ask me to trust in you. I long to do this, but I need your grace in order to do so!

There is no one as free as the one who is aware of your presence throughout the world, no one as full of peace as the one who finds reminders of you in all things, even in things made by human hands, in human cultures, and in both art and science. Until a person can do this, it doesn't matter how much knowledge one has or how affluent he or she may be. Such a person will remain spiritually blind and weak and unable to become mature in his or her faith relationship with you.

There is a big difference between the wisdom of such a devout, spiritually enlightened person, and the person who is merely highly educated. Education has its place and can be valuable when added to spiritual wisdom, but by itself it can be of little value.

People ask about a person's accomplishments, but they are not so careful about asking about that person's motives. They ask if he or she has been strong, rich, handsome or beautiful, clever, a good writer, a good singer, or a good workman or technician; but often nothing is said about his or her kindness, patience, gentleness, devotion to God, or the quality of his or her inner life. It is natural human instinct to consider outward characteristics, but grace looks at those of the spirit. Therefore, we are often mistaken in our estimation of other people, unless we are sensitive to their inner spiritual qualities.

CHAPTER 32

On Gaining True Freedom

The risen Lord speaks: My child, you cannot have complete freedom unless you seek my will alone in all things. People are in spiritual chains as long as they seek happiness and peace in the endless accumulation of possessions, place first priority on selfishly pursuing their own interests, covet what others have, and always look for the easiest way rather than the best way. For all is empty that does not come from God.

Don't be discouraged or fearful when you hear about the ways of those who have attained holiness in this world. Rather, be inspired by and learn from their example. Try each day to see reminders of me in all things and to see my presence in all times and places. True heavenly wisdom has no inflated opinion of itself and is not interested in impressing anyone but me.

On the Flighty Human Heart and on Keeping God Uppermost

The risen Lord speaks: My child, never rely on how you happen to feel at the moment, for you will soon feel quite different. Also, don't become a habitual user of mind or emotion altering substances; otherwise, you will forget how it feels to be a God-filled, normal human being. You don't need anything to "get high" except me, other people, and my creation. As long as you are alive on this earth, you will be subject to change—sometimes you will feel happy, sometimes sad; sometimes peaceful, sometimes troubled or anxious; sometimes devout, sometimes not; sometimes enthusiastic, sometimes apathetic; sometimes serious, sometimes in a silly mood. That's just the way life is.

The one who is wise and spiritually mature stands above his or her constantly shifting emotions, for how one feels is never the ultimate reality. Instead, such a person can keep his or her focus on proper longed-for goals. You can remain steady and faithful if you act on your will rather than on your feelings.

The clearer the eye of the will, the more steady you will be amid the constantly changing conditions of life. But the clear eye of the will is dim in many people because they are so ready to be distracted by any bright bauble that they happen to see. It is rare to find a person who is free from being selfish and self-centered.

To Love God Above
All Things and in All Things

The follower of Christ speaks: My God and my all, what more can I want when I have you? You are everything I could ever need or want. You are all peace and freedom.

My God and my all! This says everything for the one who understands, and for the one who loves you there is joy in repeating these words often. When we remember that you are always with us, in all times, places, and things, then all things give us delight. But when we forget about you, or our heart grows cold toward you, then there is no peace and no delight. You give the calm heart great peace and happiness. It is you from whom all peace and contentment come. Without awareness of your presence, nothing can please us for long.

Those who crave mere cleverness and "information" do not have your wisdom for the world, insofar as it turns away from you, is full of foolishness, sometimes even to the point of death. But when we are open to your love and your presence in all times, places, and things, then we fulfill our deepest nature as human beings. Then we are reoriented from falsehood to truth and from emptiness to fullness. Whenever we find the deepest good in all things, then it is you that we find. Only you, our God, taste good to us. Very different is the flavor of the created realm apart from you—time separated from eternity, and darkness without light—which is the experience of the one who lives without being open to your presence and your love.

O eternal light, brighter than all created lights and present in all created lights, purify my sight so that I may see you in all times, places, and things. Bring gladness and light into my heart so that I may hold tight to your presence in joyful ecstasy. Still, I know that I cannot have perfect joy in time and space. All the same, help me to see you and know your love often, for I have no hope and no safety except in you, my Lord and my God.

There Is No Security
in This Life Except in God

The risen Lord speaks: My child, you must know that you are never completely safe and secure in this life except insofar as you give yourself completely to me in response to my love for you. In this life, empty, self-destructive opportunities are endlessly available to you. Spend at least a few minutes each day with me in quiet prayer, listening at least as much as you yammer away to me. Fix your heart firmly to me, and then you will be secure. You must be practical about living in this world. But don't ever think that financial forms of security offer the most reliable security in this world. That would be a big mistake. Be practical and realistic when it comes to your income and dealing with finances. But trust completely in me alone. Otherwise, you will end up in misery.

CHAPTER 36

Rejection by Other People Is Unimportant

The risen Lord speaks: My child, give your heart to me and I will give you peace. Have no concern about being criticized or rejected by other people as long as your conscience assures you that you are trying to live according to the gospel. It is even good and blessed to experience such criticism and rejection, and it won't be difficult as long as you trust in God rather than in yourself.

People have many motives, some of them self-centered, when they criticize others, so don't give them any credit. Besides, it's impossible to please all of the people all of the time. Saint Paul wanted to please everyone in the Lord, and he tried to be all things to everyone (see 1 Corinthians 9:22), yet he paid little attention to what other people thought of him (see 1 Corinthians 4:3). He did all that he could for the good of others, yet he could not always avoid being criticized and rejected. So, he just gave the whole situation to God, who alone could see and understand everything. When others lied about him, he defended himself only with patience and humility. Still, he did reply to his critics sometimes, so that less mature Christians would not be disappointed or hurt by his failure to speak.

CHAPTER 37

On Giving Yourself Entirely to God in Order To Have True Freedom of Spirit

The risen Lord speaks: The way of the gospel can sometimes be difficult. The gospel requires you to give up self-centeredness so that you may find me. It requires you to give up the right to choose and to control so that you may gain all in life that truly matters. An abundant share in my risen life will be given to you the moment you surrender your own will to my will and don't try to get it back again.

I want you to give yourself entirely to me so that you may become truly who you really are meant to become. Some people surrender themselves to me but hold something back. They do not trust God totally and completely but try to take care of themselves instead of trusting God to take care of them. Such people will never gain the true freedom that belongs to those who will only one thing: my will.

I have often said it to you, and I say it again: give up self-centeredness, surrender yourself to me, and you will have the greatest peace of heart and mind possible in this world. Give your all for the One who is all. Expect nothing and you will have everything. Abandon yourself to me in all things, and without feeling sorry about it, and you will have me completely. You will then have a free heart, and darkness will not surround you. Desire to follow me and to know and do my will, and you will be alive with me forever.

Then you will be able to recognize illusions and reject them, and foolish cares will have no attraction for you. The anxieties that you cannot control will fade away, and love for things that are not worthy of your heart will fade, too.

CHAPTER 38

On Learning Self-Control and Turning to God in Difficult Times

The risen Lord speaks: My child, make it your goal to become inwardly free and to listen above all to your own conscience when it comes to making choices both great and small. Aim to have situations subject to you rather than you being subject to situations. When your choices and actions are concerned, be master of your own affairs rather than slave or servant to anyone or anything else. Be a free person, a true servant of God with the status and freedom of a child of God. See God's love reflected in all things and be on the lookout for the eternal. Dedicate yourself to serving God and doing his will in this world. Give thanks to God for all things. But always be on the alert to recognize the things of heaven in this world, too.

In all aspects of your life, don't limit your vision to superficial appearances. Instead, be on the alert for the things of God and the ways of God—in your work, in your relationships with others, in your recreation, and in all that you do and say. Turn to me in prayer often during your day, not just begging help, but giving thanks and praise, too. Always remember that God is deserving of your thanks and praise.

Don't Let Worry, Fear, and Anxiety Rule Your Life

The risen Lord speaks: My child, always and in all things give your concerns to me. When the time is right, I will work all things out to your best advantage. Be patient and wait prayerfully, and you will see that all will work out for the best for you.

The follower of Christ speaks: Lord Jesus, I want very much to trust in you, for I know that worry and fear can do me no good. If only I could stop worrying about the future and give myself over completely to your will!

The risen Lord speaks: My child, quite often people feel a deep desire for something, and they go after it with a passion. But once they have what they wanted so much, they begin to feel differently about it. It's common to never have a lasting interest in anything but to move from one thing to another. Therefore, it's important to seek my will, rather than your own, even in small matters.

In both the short and the long run, it's to your benefit to give up your own will and desires, for this is the way of true inner freedom and joy. Don't be misled by your own shifting, restless desires and fascinations but seek my will in all things. Then you will be as happy as anyone can be in this world.

CHAPTER 40

Use the Gifts That God Gives You

The follower of Christ speaks: Lord, help me to recognize, be thankful for, and use for good the gifts you have given me. What does anyone do to earn the gifts you give us, Lord? Nothing, of course. You give each person unique and special gifts, and with your grace we can use these gifts to serve you in this world. You, O Lord, are always the same. Always and forever you are good, just, holy, and true. Help me to discover and cultivate the gifts you have given me so that I may serve you and your people in this world.

Thanks be to you, for all things are sent by you. I stand before you as your servant, weak and struggling, yes, but with your help I can do much good. Help me to want to serve you more than to gain the approval and praise of other people. May your name be praised, not mine. May your works be celebrated, not mine. You are my glory, the rejoicing of my heart. In you I will rejoice all the days of my life.

Let others seek the honors that come from other people. I want to be ambitious for the honor that comes from you alone, O God, my truth, my mercy. O Blessed Trinity, to you alone be a blessing and honor and power and glory throughout endless generations. Amen.

CHAPTER 41

On Keeping Things in Perspective

The risen Lord speaks: My child, do not be concerned when others receive worldly honors while you are passed over and left in obscurity. Instead, turn your heart to me and care nothing for the honor and glory that the world offers.

The follower of Christ speaks: Lord, we are easily deceived and misguided. If I look at myself honestly, I can see that I have never truly been treated unjustly by anything in your creation, and so I have no business complaining to you about anything. I miss the mark often and, thus, have done harm to my relationships with you, with other people, and with the earth, our home. Sometimes I do rotten things. There is something to the old blues song, "It Serves Me Right to Suffer." All the same, I know that your mercy and kindness are endless, and you forgive me as many times as I turn to you with a sorrowful heart. Thus, I hope that you will give me inner peace, stability, and spiritual enlightenment to be made one with you.

Don't Let Your Peace of Mind
Depend on Other People

The risen Lord speaks: My child, if your peace depends too much on some close friend whose company gives you comfort and consolation, you will be insecure because you must rely ultimately on me alone. If you turn at all times to the everlasting, always-trustworthy God who is love, then you will not become unhappy if your friend leaves you or dies. Your love for your friend must be rooted in me, and it is for my sake that you must love any good person who is dear to you on earth. True friendship has no strength and will not last apart from me. This is even true in marriage. A marriage cannot be loving, lasting, and happy unless both spouses put all their trust in me.

You will draw closer to me the more you can find me in all things and all events in your life, whether pleasant or unpleasant. No matter what happens to you, the more you can trust in me, the more you will find meaning in life and the less you will be controlled by fear and anxiety. Learn to act in selfless ways and to act from hope rather than fear. Then you will be able to gain true knowledge of God.

CHAPTER 43

Against Useless Forms of Knowledge

The risen Lord speaks: My child, don't be too impressed by people who seem to be slick and "in control" all the time. Don't be misled by those who seem to "have it all together." Instead, pay attention to my words, for they will inspire your heart, enlighten your mind, and help you to have a life worth living.

Don't spend a lot of time reading the Scriptures just to impress other people with how much you know about the Bible. Instead, read in order to learn how to act unselfishly. Learn from me, the source of all truth, for I am the only one who can raise the humble to understanding. In my teaching there is no razzle-dazzle, no emptiness. Not everyone receives my gifts in the same ways, of course. To some I give a kind of general message, to others I speak things meant only for them. Some know my presence in signs and symbols, while others know my mysteries in ways they can hardly speak about. Even an agnostic or atheist can teach you something about me. It's important to read and learn all you can from good books. But I am within you, the truth that teaches your heart and guides your actions. I give to each one what I know he or she needs most.

CHAPTER 44

On Not Getting Too Distracted by Superficial Things

The risen Lord speaks: My child, it is better to not be concerned about things that annoy you and not to worry about people whose opinions irritate you. As long as you stand right with God and care only for what he thinks of you, then you need have no fear of anything on this earth. Don't be bothered by people whose religious views seem weird or outlandish to you, for they are my concern alone. Don't get into arguments with such people, for you will be wasting your time.

The follower of Christ speaks: Lord Jesus, what a mess we've gotten ourselves into! We whine about any threat or harm done to our material or financial situation, and we scurry about for some small gain, while we have no problem overlooking any spiritual harm we do to ourselves and others. We may work hours each day, but we also waste considerable time on diversions that do us little or no good and carelessly bypass the need to nourish our faith and our intimacy with you and with one another. Even giving a few minutes to prayer each day often seems like too much trouble for us.

CHAPTER 45

Don't Believe
Everything You Hear

The follower of Christ speaks: Lord Jesus, you are the only one who can deliver us from danger, and it's useless to put our hopes in other people. How frequently I have been disappointed when I trusted others. Still, many times I have found people to be trustworthy when I didn't expect them to be so. There's no telling what to expect! You, O God, are the only absolutely reliable one. So help me to trust in you, regardless of what the future seems to hold.

It doesn't happen often that one finds a true friend who will stand by you in all kinds of trouble. You alone, Lord Jesus, are trustworthy in all things, and no other friend can compare with you.

How true it is that the greatest wisdom is to have one's mind solidly grounded and rooted in Christ. If this were really true for me, then anxiety about other people's opinions of me would have less power over me, and I would not mind so much what other people say.

Is anyone capable of foreseeing or doing anything to avoid the darkness and injustice we see in the world? The bad that we do foresee still hurts us when it happens, so naturally the unforeseen hard times hurt us deeply, too. But why did I not do more than I did to avoid misery? Why was I so ready to believe what others said? We are still humans with all the weaknesses of humanity.

Is there anyone, Lord Jesus, I can believe and trust? Anyone, that is, but you? You are the truth, and you cannot lie or be lied to. On the other hand, humans are hard to believe and trust. People are weak, unreliable, and untrustworthy, especially when it comes to the things they say.

How wise you are to caution us to not put our complete trust in people, but only in you. Experience has taught me a good lesson, and I hope it will help me to be more cautious, not more foolish. Someone I knew once said to me, "Be careful and keep what I say to yourself." So I said nothing to anyone else, and I thought that no one else knew what I knew. But this person was himself unable to keep the secret he had asked me not to share with anyone else. Instead, he went off and blabbed to others what he had just told me to keep to myself.

Lord Jesus, protect me from careless talk and thoughtless people like this. Save me from listening to them or doing the same myself. Place true and trustworthy words in my mouth, and help me to never talk just to hear my own words or to try to impress others with nonsense. What a good thing it is if we can keep our mouths shut about other people and not believe everything others say, especially about other people. If we want to keep your divine life alive in us, the best way to act is to avoid all that is most impressive in the eyes of the popular culture and, instead of striving for what attracts other people's admiration, to make every effort to become a good and sensible person of faith, hope, and charitable love.

CHAPTER 46

On Trusting Firmly in God
When Wild Talk Happens All Around You

The risen Lord speaks: My child, remain firm in faith and put your hope in me. After all, words are only words—they fly through the air, but they do not hurt anything that is solid. If you did something wrong, just say to yourself, *I am sorry, and I'll gladly correct my faults.* If you did nothing wrong and your conscience accuses you of nothing, say, *I will gladly put up with being unjustly accused for God's sake.* It is no big deal if you sometimes must tolerate harsh words from others. The only reason such a little thing bothers you so much is that you are still ruled by your old, superficial self and you take more notice of what other people say than you should. Because you are afraid of other people's contempt, you don't want to be corrected when you make a mistake, and you try to cover up by making excuses.

Listen to my word, and you will have no concern about thousands of words from other people. Remember that I am the one who knows you in truth, and I do not judge by appearances. Often what people think is praiseworthy is silly in my sight.

The follower of Christ speaks: O Lord God, judge me in truth, you who know the weakness and failures of humankind. Be my strength and confidence, for my own ways of looking at things easily lead me astray. You know what I don't know. Be gracious and forgive me for all the times I have not acted in truth and in the spirit of the gospel. For it is better to leave it to your great mercy to forgive me than to insist on my imaginary innocence and stifle my carefully hidden sense of guilt. Help me to remember that sometimes guilt is a perfectly appropriate feeling.

CHAPTER 47

All Kinds of Hardships Are Worth Enduring for the Sake of Eternal Life

The risen Lord speaks: My child, don't let yourself be exhausted or totally stressed out by the work you do for my sake, but always let my presence in your deepest center give you strength, comfort, and hope. Believe me, I can reward you far beyond your wildest dreams. Your work here won't last very long, and you won't always be weighed down with anxiety and concern. The time will come when all your effort and persistence will come to an end, and anything that passes with time isn't worth worrying about.

Do the best you can at what you're doing, work faithfully for me, and I will be your reward. Love God with your whole being. Remain faithful to your most basic life commitments, whatever they are. Be a faithful friend to others, especially those who have special needs. Eternal life is worth all this and more.

On the Eternal Day and the Difficulties of This Life

The follower of Christ speaks: The days of our existence in time and space are brief and filled with joy and love sometimes, dissatisfaction and frustration at other times. When will all be love and joy? When will I know continuous peace, peace that cannot be taken from me, peace within and peace without, peace all around me? O blessed heavenly home, how I long for you! O eternal day filled with light streaming from the Truth, how I yearn for you! There I will be forever happy and free from fear.

Comfort and strengthen me, good Lord Jesus, and help me to remain faithful to you during my pilgrimage to full union with you. Help me to love God and neighbor at all times, especially when it is difficult to do so.

CHAPTER 49

On Desiring Eternal Life and the Great Rewards Promised to Those Who Remain Faithful

The risen Lord speaks: My child, I know that sometimes you long for eternal happiness with me even now during your time on earth. Turn to me, then, and open your heart, and I will give you comfort and encouragement so that you can do my work.

Don't ask only for what you find easy and fun, but ask for what pleases and honors me. If you have your priorities straight, you will prefer my will to your own wants and wishes. I know what you want. I hear your begging and pleading. You would like to have a life that is easy and comfortable. But I had no such life, so why should you expect a life any different if you would be my friend and follower?

When you don't want to do something for my sake and for the

sake of your neighbor, you need to put your old self behind you. Think of the reward you will receive, beginning even now, when you do my will. So be ready and willing to do what needs to be done for God and neighbor. Let other people set their hearts on all kinds of empty goals. Your only desire must be to love God and serve your neighbor in loving charity. The one thing worth desiring is to bring attention to God's great love in this world.

CHAPTER 50

When You're Not at Peace, Abandon Yourself to God's Love

The follower of Christ speaks: God, in your will is our only good. May all your servants find their joy in you, not in themselves or in any created thing as an end in itself. You alone are my true happiness; you are my hope and ultimate reward. I have no powers or gifts that did not come from you. All things belong to you.

Sometimes I feel so down and discouraged, and my troubles threaten to overwhelm me. I want so much to know your joy and peace. Help me to never give up my hope in you and to never lose my trust in your loving care. I thank you from the bottom of my heart for your mercy, compassion, and forgiveness, and for rescuing me from my old self and the stupid and self-destructive choices I have made in the past.

Help me, O Lord, to know what I need to know and love what I ought to love so that I may praise what most pleases you, value only what is precious in your sight, and reject all that you reject. Help me never to judge by appearances or to base my opinions on mere rumors or hearsay. Rather, give me discernment and right judgment in all things. Help me to seek your will above all things. Human judgments are often mistaken, and those who do not seek you are often misled by their craving for the comforts and security of this world. Does it make anyone a better person when he or she is thought highly of by other people? Rather, a person is what he or she appears in the eyes of God, and not one bit more or less.

Keep on With Humble Good Works
When You Can't Do Great Things

The risen Lord speaks: My child, there is no way you can be filled with ecstatic joy all the time. It's just not possible for human nature always to feel this way. As long as you are in time and space, you will sometimes feel restless, sometimes discouraged, and sometimes down. You may be tempted to abuse drugs or alcohol, but there is nothing but misery down that path no matter what anyone else tells you. When you're feeling sad or just ordinary, the best thing to do is to occupy yourself quietly with your daily work and to turn to me from time to time with a momentary prayerful thought. Before long, you will feel better and become aware of my presence again. You will remember that I am always closer to you than you are to yourself, no matter how you are feeling.

Remember that you can always refresh your heart by finding me in the green fields of the Scriptures. Remember that I am always ready to give myself to you in the sacraments of the Church, especially in holy Communion and reconciliation. Receive these sacraments often. The path I have set for you is wide open before you when you turn often to the sacraments and the Scriptures.

CHAPTER 52

Consider Yourself Blessed,
No Matter What Happens to You

The follower of Christ speaks: Sometimes I get so down on myself, Lord Jesus, and I feel worthless and without any hope for the future. Help me at such times to turn to you and remember your great love for me. Help me to remember that you need me to be your ambassador and disciple in this world, to do your work in many small ways each day. Indeed, if I don't do what I can, who will?

You, O God, are merciful and compassionate, and you do not want what you have created to be destroyed. Instead, you want to display in those to whom you show your mercy how great your goodness is. Naturally, I can never deserve it. But that doesn't matter to you, so you give me your mercy and comfort without measure.

What have I ever done, Lord, to deserve your great love and mercy? As far I can tell, I haven't done a single thing. Instead, I'm always ready to make self-destructive choices or choices that harm my relationships with others and with you. I'm always slow to change my ways. That's the pure truth, and I can't deny it. And all I get from you in return is greater mercy, forgiveness, and love. All I can say is, Lord, have mercy on me. Into your hands I commend myself entirely, both now and forever.

The only thing you ask of us is regret for our mistakes and stupid choices and the willingness to turn back to you time after time. For where there is a sincere desire to return to you, the hope of mercy returns and the troubled conscience finds peace. Lost peace is restored, and you, O God, run to meet and embrace us with a loving kiss before we can even knock on your door. How mind-boggling is this?

CHAPTER 53

The Grace of God Must Be Sought Before All

The risen Lord speaks: My child, my divine life given to you, my grace, is the most precious gift there is, and it's all for you at all times and in all places. You may discover me in any situation and any circumstances. I am close to you in and through creation, in your relationships with others, and in your troubles and difficulties. I am present to you in your marriage if you are married; in the circumstances of your single life if you are unmarried; in your life as a celibate priest if you are a priest; and in every aspect of your personal and community life if you are a vowed religious. No matter who you are or what your state in life is, I am there sharing with you my divine life, my grace, as long as you are open to my presence.

You can come to the end of your life with confidence when you have lived in communion with me in all kinds of situations and circumstances. Always seek me rather than the things of the world. If you have lived with me, you need have no anxiety about dying with me. People get into trouble only when they refuse to overcome selfishness and do not try wholeheartedly to leave their old selves behind. If you want to live in freedom with me, it is essential that you seek me in all situations and circumstances and strive to overcome your natural inclination to be self-centered.

CHAPTER 54

How We Are Affected by Our Old Selves and Our New Selves

The risen Lord speaks: My child, be watchful when it comes to how your old self and your new self—the new you that was born in baptism—affect your life, choices, and behavior. The old self is cunning and can mislead you because it always has its own interests at heart. However, grace, my divine life in you, aims to quietly, gently, lead the old self to give all over to the new self, which desires nothing but God's will in all things.

The old self works for its own benefit and tries to take advantage of others. The new self has no concern for its personal convenience and advantage but rather what will do most good for others. The old self is always ready to accept honor and respect, but the new self always attributes all honor and glory to God alone. The old self likes idleness and physical comfort, but the new self gladly works faithfully for the glory of God in this world.

The old self has its eye on material things without being aware of their status as gifts from God meant to be used for the good of others and the glory of God. In material loss, the new self feels no distress or anxiety, for its treasure is with Christ. The old self takes great offense when others are inconsiderate or mean. In the same situation, the new self feels no resentment or sadness, for its joy is with Christ. As the old self is calmed and its fears allayed, the new self develops more fully, and the inward person is daily transformed in Christ and remade in the image and likeness of God.

CHAPTER 55

On the Uselessness of the Old Self and on the Power of Grace

The follower of Christ speaks: God, who created me from nothing in your own image and likeness, grant me the fullness of your divine life and your Holy Spirit so that I might be saved. For I am always aware of an inclination toward fear, anxiety, and self-destructive behavior on the part of my old self. I have no power to resist this inclination without the help of your holy life, your grace, burning within my heart.

O Lord, I need your life within me so much if I am to accomplish any good in this world. Without grace there is no way I can do anything. On the other hand, with your grace giving me light and strength, nothing is beyond my powers—nothing!

True grace of God's life within our hearts! Without it, personal accomplishments and natural talents are of no use. Wealth and talent, good looks and physical strength, intellectual abilities, and being good with words have no value apart from your grace in us. For natural talents are common to both those who are good and those who are bad alike. But grace, your divine life and love within us, is found only in those who accept the gift of loving intimacy with you, O God.

Blessed grace of God's life in us! You make the poor in spirit rich in goodness, and rich people you make humble in their hearts. Come to me, and pour out your comfort and encouragement on me very soon, or my soul will grow weary and give up.

Lord Jesus, please look on me with mercy, for your grace is enough for me. Your grace takes away fear and anxiety. It teaches us the truth, gives light to our hearts, brings comfort in hard times, and comforts us in our sorrows. Without your grace, I am like dead wood, a useless stump, fit only to be ground into sawdust.

So, God, may your divine life in me, your grace, always go before me and protect me from behind. May it enable me to give myself constantly to good works of loving charity, through Jesus Christ, your Son. Amen.

CHAPTER 56

We Must Reject Selfishness and Follow Christ With His Cross

The risen Lord speaks: My child, you can only enter into complete intimacy with me insofar as you are able to forget your old self. Follow me, the way, the truth, and the life (see John 14:6). For without the way, you cannot travel; without the truth you can know nothing worth knowing; and without the life, you can have no life worth living. I am the way you must follow, the truth you must trust and believe, the life you must welcome into your heart. I am the way that cannot become lost, the truth that can never lead you wrong, the life that can never end. I am the straightest way, the highest truth, the life that is most blessed. If you really want to experience true life now and someday to enter into eternal life, then keep the commandments and meditate upon the gospels.

The follower of Christ speaks: Lord Jesus, help me to one day see your promises fulfilled in my life. I have taken up my cross, and I take it from your hand. I will carry it for every day of my life in obedience to your teaching. How true it is that no one can experience your resurrection unless we also take up your cross.

Come along then, my fellow disciples of the risen Christ, let us move ahead together, for the Lord Jesus is always with us. Our leader marches on ahead of us, and he will help and guide us. Let us follow him boldly, without fear, ready to do whatever is required by faith in him.

CHAPTER 57

A Caution Against Getting Too Discouraged When Life Seems Too Difficult

The risen Lord speaks: My child, it's better to be patient and humble when your life is difficult than to be filled with devotion and spiritual joy when your life is easy. Don't let yourself be unhappy when some little thing goes wrong. Even if it were something big, it shouldn't upset you. As it is, just let it go. It is nothing new, and it's not the first time such a thing has happened. And you can bet your bottom dollar it won't be the last time, either.

You are strong enough as long as no trouble comes your way. You are also pretty good at giving advice to and offering words of comfort to others. But when some unexpected trouble comes knocking at your own door, well, then your good advice and words of comfort vanish into thin air. Pay attention to your own weakness, which appears whenever you have problems or trouble of any kind. Remember that troubles and anxieties give you an opportunity to let your faith become real.

Whatever trouble you are having, usher it to the door of your heart and show it out as best you can. Even if it does touch you deeply, don't let it depress you or worry you for too long. If you find yourself feeling depressed or gloomy most of the time, then for heaven's sake find someone who can help you to mediate God's grace to you—perhaps a wise counselor or gifted therapist. All the commotion that has been stirred up in your deepest center will soon go away, and your inner darkness will soon turn to light by the renewal of grace, God's life in you. For I am still living in you, and I am ready to help you and comfort you more than you can begin to imagine if you trust in me and call on me.

Take things in your life more calmly and brace yourself to put up with difficulties without letting them get you down. Remember that you are human, not an angel. How do you think you can be perfect when it was impossible for Adam and Eve and even for the angels in heaven? I always offer comfort and consolation to those who turn to me.

The follower of Christ speaks: Lord, what you have said to me is truly blessed. Your guidance is sweeter to my taste than honey from the honeycomb. What would I do in the midst of all my troubles and worries without the comfort and encouragement of your words? What would I do without the Bread of Life in holy Communion and without the healing and comfort of the sacrament of reconciliation? When my days come to a conclusion, Lord, help me to have a good death and grant me a happy passage from this world into eternity. Remember me, Lord, and guide me by a straight path to your heavenly home. Amen.

CHAPTER 58

On Not Trying to Understand More Than Your Mind Can Grasp

The risen Lord speaks: My child, it's important to use the intellect God gave you. True faith is never blind. For example, as I have said before, it's nearly as important to read about the Scriptures as it is to read the Scriptures themselves. Only when you have an accurate understanding of what the Bible is, where it came from, and what its purposes are, can you read and understand it accurately and without ending up with some out-of-kilter ideas. It's also important to be a lifelong learner when it comes to understanding your religion and your faith. Ignorance is no virtue!

Given all this, however, it's also important to realize that the human mind has limitations and that you'll never completely understand all the mysteries of life and all the mysteries of faith. If you find yourself thinking that maybe the only kind of knowledge worth accepting is scientific knowledge, remind yourself that even science cannot prove that the only valid knowledge is scientific knowledge. People who believe this can only do so by taking it on a kind of "faith."

Ultimately, everything is incomprehensible to the human intellect but not to the human heart. The main thing is what you do when your mind reaches its limits: believe or disbelieve? Faith or faithlessness? Those are your choices. To paraphrase Blaise Pascal, the seventeenth-century French Catholic mathematician and philosopher, the heart has its reasons that the intellect knows nothing about. The knowledge that comes from the heart is just as valid as the knowledge that comes from the intellect.

So, my child, use your intellect to its maximum. But don't expect undeniable scientific proof of the existence of God. If science could prove God's existence, that would mean that the finite human mind could grasp the infinite God, which would mean that God, the Divine Mystery, would be no mystery at all. Only love and the human heart can fully grasp God.

CHAPTER 59

Trust and Hope
in God Alone

The follower of Christ speaks: Lord, I would rather be in poverty and close to you than surrounded by riches and comfort without your presence. I would rather wander the earth and feel you close to me than have wealth and a huge, beautiful home and never know your presence. Where you are there heaven is, too. In all my longings it is you, ultimately, that I long for. There is no one but you, my God, on whom I can rely to be with me and help me in my needs. You are my hope and confidence, my comforter. You are always faithful in all things.

Most people have only their own interests at heart, but you want nothing but my good, my healing and liberation, and my progress. Wherever I look apart from you, I find weakness and unreliability.

And so, God, in you I find my own hope and my only home, and with you I leave all my troubles and my sorrows.

Bless me and sanctify my deepest inner self, O Lord, with the blessings of heaven so that I will remember that I am your dwelling place and that you are always closer to me than I am to myself. Hear the prayer of your servant as I travel through this world of light and darkness. Protect and preserve me amid the dangers of this life. Send your divine life, your grace, to accompany me and guide me by the paths of peace until I arrive at the land of never-fading light and goodness. Amen.

BOOK IV

Reflections
On the Eucharist

The voice of Christ:

"*Come to me, all you that are weary and are carrying heavy burdens, and I will give you rest.*"

MATTHEW 11:28

"*...the bread that I will give for the life of the world is my flesh.*"

JOHN 6:51

"*Take and eat, this is my body, which is being given for you. Do this in remembrance of me.*"

SEE MATTHEW 26:26 AND 1 CORINTHIANS 11:24

"*Those who eat my flesh and drink my blood abide in me, and I in them.*"

JOHN 6:56

CHAPTER 1

Receive the Risen Christ
With Reverence

The follower of Christ speaks: Lord Jesus, eternal truth, these words are yours, even though they come from various places in the Scriptures. They are your words, and they are true, and so I accept them with gratitude and joy. They are your words given in the holy Scriptures. They are mine, too, because you spoke them for my salvation. I receive your words with gladness so that they may fill my heart.

And yet, Lord Jesus, I know also that these words of yours come from long ago and far away. I know that language changes, and sometimes we can misunderstand words spoken long ago and miss their real and richest meaning. So I have studied on your words, Lord, and now know more than I once did about their meaning.

When you say that you give us your body and blood to eat, this was how in your time on this earth people expressed the idea of "the whole self." So in saying that you give us your body and blood to eat, we need to understand today that you are saying that you give us your "whole self" to eat. What a great blessing and a great gift this is for us, Lord Jesus! When we receive holy Communion, we receive your whole self as our nourishment on our pilgrimage.

But I know, Lord Jesus, that there is even more than this to your gift of yourself to us in the Mass. For it is not just your earthly self that we receive. It is you as you are now, in your risen, heavenly form that we receive! What a great and glorious mystery is your gift to us in holy Communion! Help me to approach and receive your whole risen self in holy Communion with joy and with reverence, Lord, for no gift on earth can compare with this one.

Lord Jesus, help me also to be mindful of your presence in the eucharistic bread that is kept in the tabernacles of our churches and that is adored during exposition of the Blessed Sacrament. You, the Risen Lord, are with us always to remind us of your presence in us and in our gatherings.

The Eucharist Reveals
God's Great Goodness and Love

The follower of Christ speaks: Trusting in your great goodness and mercy, Lord, I come to you. World weary, hungry and thirsty for your divine life, I come to the well of life. Needy, I come to the Lord of heaven; a servant, I turn to my master; a creature, I turn to my maker; full of anxiety and sorrow, I come to him who loves, comforts, and encourages me.

Lord Jesus, risen Christ, what reverence and gratitude we owe you for giving us your risen self, complete, in the Eucharist. No one can comprehend the greatness of this mystery!

Lord of all, it was your choice to nourish our loving intimacy by the Eucharist. By means of this sacrament, forgive all the ways in which I have chosen to harm my relationships with other people, with the earth, and with you. Heal me by means of this sacrament so that I may renew my dedication to serving you and your people in this world.

The risen Lord speaks: Whenever you participate in a celebration of the Mass, strive to participate fully and not as a mere observer. Think about this great mystery that nourishes your faith and your love for God and neighbor. Whenever you participate in the Mass, it should seem as new, as wonderful, and as joyful to you as if on this very day Christ first came into the world to live, die, and to rise for the sake of our liberation and healing in this world and in eternity.

CHAPTER 3

It Is a Great Help to Participate in the Mass Frequently

The follower of Christ speaks: See, Lord, I come to you so that I may be blessed and made glad at the sacred banquet where you give abundant gifts to your loved ones. You are my salvation and strength, O Lord.

Comfort your servant's heart today, Lord. I want nothing more than to participate fully in the celebration of the Eucharist and to receive your whole risen self with reverence and devotion. Give yourself to me and I will be satisfied, for nothing other than you can really comfort me.

I cannot exist without you, and without your presence I have no strength to live from day to day. Therefore, I must come to your Eucharist and receive you often for my healing, nourishment, and salvation. So often I fail and make bad or inappropriate choices. I so easily give up hope, and so I must pray often, confess my sinfulness, and receive your holy self, risen and in glory, so that I may be cleansed, renewed, and inspired again. Holy Communion serves to bring me back to yourself and back to your ways. It refreshes my heart and renews my faith and hope.

CHAPTER 4

Many Blessings Come to Those Who Receive Holy Communion Devoutly

The follower of Christ speaks: Lord Jesus, risen Christ, come to meet your servant with the blessings of your goodness and divine life so that I may be able to participate in the Mass prayerfully, actively, and with reverence and receive holy Communion happily.

Fill my heart with love for you and for my neighbor whom you call me to love with charitable compassion. Give light to my eyes so that I may recognize your divine presence. Strengthen my loving intimacy with you. For in the Eucharist you are at work with a far more than human power. It is your holy liturgy and no work of mere human imagination.

It is your will that I receive you and become one with you in love. Therefore, I pray for your mercy and ask you to grant me the special grace of being united with you now and in eternity. This sacrament is all I need to be faithful to you. It is the health of soul and body and nourishment for the way. By it faith is increased, hope is strengthened, and love is kindled to encompass my entire being.

Whatever I need, Lord Jesus, please provide for me by means of this wonderful sacrament. There is no one to help me but you, no one to set me free but you. I give myself entirely to you that you may watch over me and guide me in all things. Receive me as I, having been invited by you, receive your risen self in holy Communion. Lord Jesus, risen Savior, grant that as the mystery of the Eucharist is repeated time and again in my life, so may my love and devotion to you and to your people grow and increase.

CHAPTER 5

The Dignity of the Blessed Sacrament and of the Priesthood

The follower of Christ speaks: By ourselves, no one is truly worthy to receive or celebrate the sacrament of the Eucharist. It is only because we have been brought into the life of Christ by the grace of God through the sacrament of baptism that we are worthy to participate in and receive the Eucharist. The priest, by virtue of his baptism and the graces received through the sacrament of holy orders, presides at the table of the Lord for the sake of the entire eucharistic assembly.

The priest needs to remember that he must preside with reverence and respect. It is never the place of the priest to impose his personal spirituality on the entire assembly by changing or modifying the ritual in ways that merely reflect his personal piety or theological opinions. Instead, he must limit himself to presiding at the Eucharist in those ways provided for the good of the entire assembly and express his own piety and opinions at other times and places.

Indeed, the personality of the priest should have but a minor impact on the Liturgy of the Eucharist, to the point that he should become, as it were, "transparent" to the eucharistic ritual itself. It is, of course, proper that the personality of the priest come through in appropriate ways during the homily. But no priest should preside at the table of the Lord in ways that draw attention to himself. The priest is not an entertainer. He is but the servant of God and of the eucharistic assembly—a great honor, to be sure, but not one that should lead to self-aggrandizement.

CHAPTER 6

How Can We Prepare to Participate in the Eucharist?

The follower of Christ speaks: Lord Jesus, so often I take the Eucharist for granted. Sometimes I even find it less than inspiring. O God, you are my helper and my counselor. What am I to do? Teach my heart in right ways. Show me some simple exercise to help me prepare myself suitably to participate in the celebration of the Eucharist and to receive holy Communion.

The risen Christ speaks: When you are going to participate in the Mass, remember that it is your entire life and all your experiences that you bring to the eucharistic assembly. The Mass is the summit and source of the Christian life, not something set apart from it.

If you can, and your life permits, try to look over the readings from the Lectionary that will be proclaimed at the Mass in which your will participate. If possible, and your life permits, try to arrive a few minutes before the Mass begins, so you may greet at least a few of the others who will be celebrating the Eucharist with you. Also, take a few moments to re-collect yourself in preparation for the Mass to begin.

Once the Mass begins, try to focus on each prayer and each gesture. Listen closely when the word of God is proclaimed and be attentive to the homily. Try to participate consciously and fully as the Eucharist unfolds. When it is time to receive holy Communion, do so with devotion, bowing devoutly toward the consecrated bread and wine prior to receiving each. Remember what a great privilege it is to participate in the Mass, and take advantage of every opportunity to do so, giving thanks to God at all times.

CHAPTER 7

The Life, Death, and Resurrection of Christ and Our Surrender of Ourselves

The risen Christ speaks: I freely and willingly entered into time and space, fully human and fully divine, to fulfill the will of my Father and to bring healing and liberation to all. Each time you celebrate the Eucharist, you also should freely offer yourself as my servant who brings my presence and actions into your small corner of the world each and every day. But remember, too, that above all what I want is not that you work wonders but that you give yourself entirely to me. Let me take care of the rest.

If you possessed all the things you so often want, including wealth and all the kinds of security the world offers, you still would not be satisfied without me. Offer yourself to me and give your whole self to God, our loving father, and all will be well. If you want to receive God's own life and complete freedom, then making a free gift of yourself to God must be the focus of your life at all times. Relatively few people gain enlightenment and freedom because they do not give themselves up entirely to me.

Here is a central part of my teaching in all times and all places: "So therefore, none of you can become my disciple if you do not give up all your possessions" (Luke 14:33). And although my words refer in a certain sense to material possessions—detachment from things of the world is necessary for freedom—they refer even more importantly to intangible possessions such as your opinions and prejudices and your belief in your own righteousness.

There is no sacrifice more acceptable to God than for you to give yourself entirely to me, especially during the Mass. If you do your best, truly abandon and sacrifice your self-righteousness, and approach me for grace and forgiveness, I will say: "I, I am HE / who blots out your transgressions for my own sake, / and I will not remember your sins" (Isaiah 43:25).

CHAPTER 8

Christ's Offering of Himself and Our Offering of Ourselves

The risen Christ speaks: In my public ministry, in my suffering and dying on the cross, and in my resurrection, I willingly offered myself to God, our loving father, for you and for your healing and liberation in this life and the next. Likewise, you must willingly offer yourself and your life to me in service to God and neighbor. I ask nothing less of you than the complete gift of yourself. This is what you must do if you want to receive grace and attain freedom and enlightenment. If you want to be my disciple, offer yourself to me with your whole heart.

Giving Ourselves and All We Have to God and Praying for Others

The follower of Christ speaks: Lord, everything on earth and in the heavens belongs to you. I want to give myself entirely to you. I sincerely give myself to you this day as your servant now and always. Receive me as I celebrate with the entire assembly your holy Eucharist, in the company of your angels and saints, that this Mass may help my healing and liberation in this world and the next, and that of all your people and all of your creation.

What can I do about my sins—all those ways I have damaged my relationship with you and with my neighbors and friends and all the ways I have done harm to the earth our home? I can only confess humbly, be truly sorry, beg for your forgiveness, and do what I can to heal and repair what I have damaged.

At the same time, Lord Jesus, I offer you all the good I have done thus far in my life. I thank you for your gifts that make it possible for me to do good. Take all that I am and lead me to a blessed and happy end in and with you.

Likewise, I give you all the worthy desires that all your holy people cherish in their hearts, plus the needs of all those I love and care for and all who are dear to me. May they all know protection from all danger and freedom from hard times and ill health and, being rescued from all such darkness, may they give you endless thanks.

I give you, too, my prayers and the prayers of this Mass for anyone and everyone who may have offended or hurt me or brought me some loss or injury. Likewise, I offer my prayers and this Mass for all those whom I have hurt, offended, or injured in any way, even without knowing that I did so.

Lord Jesus, empty my heart of all bitterness, suspicion, conflict, and anything that can damage loving charity and spiritual wellness in the community of faith. Have great mercy, Lord Jesus, on all those who seek your mercy! Give the gift of your divine life, your grace, to those who need it, and may we all make steady progress on our way to eternal life with you! Amen.

CHAPTER 10

Don't Put Off Participating in the Eucharist and Receiving Holy Communion

The risen Lord speaks: If you seek healing and liberation and want to be stronger and more capable of loving charity, then you must participate often in the Mass. Conscious of the great benefits of this sacrament, resist your inclination toward spiritual laziness, participate in the Mass, and often receive the whole risen self of the Lord Jesus in holy Communion.

Some people, when they think about participating in the Eucharist, find themselves feeling lazy and think of staying home instead for no good reason. Ignore such lazy inclinations. Also, avoid overly scrupulous thoughts you may have about being "unworthy" to receive holy Communion. Confess your sins and trust in God's mercy to forgive them. Remember that we celebrate the Eucharist as an instrument of God's mercy, forgiveness, and healing.

How small is the love and how filled with hopelessness are the hearts of those who put off participation in the Mass and receiving holy Communion. But how happy and blessed are those who receive holy Communion whenever they can. As often as you participate in this mystical experience and receive this mystical Communion, so often do you awaken in your heart the life, death, and resurrection of Christ and renew in your heart your love for him.

CHAPTER 11

The Eucharist and the Holy Scriptures Are Necessary to Authentic Faith

The follower of Christ speaks: Lord Jesus Christ, what great encouragement and comfort come to those who participate in the Eucharist often. Because I must be content in this world with the true light of faith and wait until eternity to see and know you directly, the need for your sacraments and for the holy Scriptures remains throughout my life. From your Eucharist I receive the food I need to live in you; and from the Scriptures I gain the light I need to follow your way. Without these two I cannot live as I should. Holy Communion is the bread of eternal life and the Word of God is light for my heart and soul.

CHAPTER 12

Don't Give in to Useless Curiosity and Questions About the Eucharist

The risen Lord speaks: Don't let your intellect suggest to you that the knowledge that comes from your heart, or deepest center, is not true knowledge, especially as regards the Eucharist. By all means become as theologically well informed as you can about the Mass. Most important, however, is a simplicity of heart that welcomes the Eucharist as the great and good mystery that it is, a mystery that conveys God's infinite love, compassion, and healing.

Therefore, continue in your adult faith (that is, loving intimacy with Christ), participate in the Mass, and receive holy Communion at every opportunity. Ask questions about the Eucharist only as you would ask questions about the love of one who loves you without reservation. For the human intellect has its limits and can be fulfilled by the knowledge that only the heart can give. When it comes to the Eucharist, loving intimacy with Christ is of utmost importance, and this loving intimacy operates in ways that the intellect can only know so much about.

The eternal God, who is in and yet beyond time, space, and all of his Creation, accomplishes wonderful, great, and mysterious things in both heaven and on earth. If the works of God were easy for the human intellect to grasp, then they could not be called great and wonderful, and they wouldn't be beyond describing. Therefore, they would not be worth believing in, would they?